I0762585

Is Everybody Ready For The Next Band?

THE ROLLING STONES 1969 US TOUR

Is Everybody Ready For The Next Band?

THE ROLLING STONES 1969 US TOUR

Richard Houghton

Spenwood Books
Manchester, UK

First published in Great Britain 2025 by Spenwood Books Ltd

1 Totnes Road, Manchester, M21 8XF, United Kingdom

A CIP record for this book is available from the British Library.

ISBN 978-1-915858-56-6

Design by Bruce Graham, The Night Owl

ABOUT THE AUTHOR

Richard Houghton lives in Manchester with his wife Kate and his dog Sid. He is the author of more than 20 books on music. The Rolling Stones are his favourite band.

INTRODUCTION

Everybody seems to be ready… Is everybody ready for the next band?

In 1969, the Rolling Stones were back in live action following a two-year hiatus brought on by a combination of drugs, police persecution of the band and a general 'we need to spend more time in the studio attitude' that The Beatles, following their retirement from live performance, had engendered.

The first step to getting road ready was 'what to do about Brian?' With his criminal record Brian Jones was not going to get a visa to tour the United States, and the Stones knew that touring the US was vital to regaining artistic credibility and throwing off their image as a sixties hits band loved by teeny boppers, and to making serious money. The Stones had two new albums to promote – *Beggar's Banquet* and the soon-to-be-released *Let It Bleed* – and Brian was, immigration problems or not, in no fit state to tour.

8 JUNE 1969

COTCHFORD FARM
HARTFIELD
EAST SUSSEX
UK

"We took his one thing away, which was being in a band"

CHARLIE WATTS

Mick Jagger, Keith Richards and Charlie Watts visit Brian Jones at his home at Cotchford Farm in East Sussex, previously owned by AA Milne of *Winnie The Pooh* fame, to break the news that the band that he founded no longer wants him to be a part of it.

KEITH RICHARDS

The fact that he was expecting it made it easier, you know, he wasn't even surprised. I didn't really think he took it all in. He was already… up in the stratosphere.

BRIAN JONES

I no longer see eye-to-eye with the others over the discs we are cutting.
(Press statement, 9 June 1969)

13 JUNE 1969

HYDE PARK
LONDON
UK

"How do I feel about joining the Rolling Stones? I'm happy to be joining them. I think it'll go really well when we start working"

MICK TAYLOR

Mick Taylor is unveiled as Brian's replacement and the Stones announce that his first show will be a free concert headlined by the Stones in London's Hyde Park on 5 July 1969. (*Rolling Stone* magazine erroneously reports that Taylor will make his debut as the Stones' new guitarist at two concerts at the Colosseum in Rome.)

3 JULY 1969

COTCHFORD FARM
HARTFIELD
EAST SUSSEX
UK

"I am just so unhappy. I am so shocked and wordless and so sad. Something has gone. I have really lost something. We were like a pack, one family in a way"

MICK JAGGER

Brian Jones is found dead in his swimming pool. There is talk of cancelling the concert planned for the coming Saturday in Hyde Park but instead it is decided to go ahead, making it a memorial concert for Brian.

5 JULY 1969

HYDE PARK
LONDON
UK

"Brian will be at the concert. I mean, he'll be there! But it all depends on what you believe in. If you're agnostic, he's just dead, and that's it. When we get there this afternoon, he's gonna be there. I don't believe in Western bereavement. You know, I can't suddenly drape a long black veil and walk the hills. But it is still very upsetting. I want to make it so that Brian's send-off from the world is filled with as much happiness as possible"

MICK JAGGER

"The all-important thing for us was it was our first appearance for a long time and with a change of personnel. It was Mick Taylor's first gig. We were going to do it anyway. Obviously, a statement had to be made of one kind or another, so we turned it into a memorial for Brian. We wanted to see him off in grand style. The ups and downs with the guy are one thing, but when his time's over, release the doves.

Or, in this case, the sackfuls of white butterflies"

KEITH RICHARDS

BRENDA PARKER

Hyde Park was like closing a chapter and turning the page and moving on into a new and very different decade. Everything had changed by then. It wasn't pop music anymore. Now it was rock, and the Stones truly were 'The Greatest Rock 'n' Roll Band in the World'. The screaming had mercifully stopped and the music was being taken seriously now. Brian's recent departure had been a blow, but word was that he was putting his own band together so that was something to look forward to, and the announcement that the Stones would do a free concert to introduce his replacement was met with great excitement.

My friend Robert and I were eager to see what the new Stones would be like, but Mick Taylor's debut was completely overshadowed by the terrible news of Brian's death, and at first no one seemed to know if the concert would take place. When word came that it was going on as planned, albeit now as a tribute to Brian, I felt it was the right thing to do. It was such a strange and surreal day, firstly because the weather was so hot, secondly because I think we were all still trying to process that Brian was dead. We weren't used to our rock stars dying then. Brian was the first, so it was truly shocking.

I remember coming out of Marble Arch Tube station and seeing a veritable army of us, all in our hippie finery streaming across Park Lane from every direction, heading into the park. I was directly behind someone dressed head to toe in heavy black velvet, maybe in mourning for Brian, and I remember thinking, 'She's going to be so uncomfortable in such a heavy outfit in all this heat.'

I don't remember what time the concert was scheduled to begin, but Robert and I got there only a couple of hours before the allotted time and had no trouble finding a place to sit, only a few yards from where the stage was being set up. Everything was so much simpler then – can you imagine doing that now? Then we just sat there and waited for what seemed like forever.

Looking back on it, I can't believe we sat there for all those hours in the boiling heat with no food or drink. And if there were bathrooms set up anywhere, I don't remember seeing them. Yet it didn't bother us at all. As time passed, we could see we'd been joined by heaven only knows how many thousands of people, some of whom had climbed trees way behind us. It was literally a sea of people, but everyone was friendly and good natured, although the mood was subdued because of Brian. At the sides of the stage the crew had set up a pair of massive pictures of Brian from the photo session for the inner sleeve of *Beggar's Banquet*, which I thought was an odd choice, but he had a big grin on his face, so I guess that's why they'd been chosen.

It took forever before the Stones finally showed up, and before they did we had to endure the Battered Ornaments, The Third Eye Band (or maybe the Third Ear Band? They were so boring I really didn't pay much attention to their name), and Alexis Korner and the New Church, who I found very disappointing. Apparently, King Crimson also played, although I have no recollection of them.

I remember seeing Marsha Hunt in the area just in front of the stage, all dressed in white-fringed buckskin and looking fabulous, but none of us knew then about the affair she was having with Mick. The security people made her move, and she was obviously annoyed – apparently the security people didn't know about the affair either!

The security people were a bunch of bikers and I've always thought it was because they did the security at this concert that the notoriously bad decision was made to use bikers as security at Altamont. The Brit bikers were pretty harmless, but I don't think anyone realised the Hell's Angels in California were just a bunch of vicious thugs and nothing like their UK counterparts.

After what seemed like a really, really long time, Sam Cutler finally announced the Stones and out came Mick in his Mr Fish white 'dress'. Knock-offs showed up in the Oxford Street boutiques within days. He looked very serious and said he was going to say a few words for Brian and read a poem by Shelley, but the sound system wasn't great. I think a lot of people thought he said he was going to read a poem by Che. And then the white butterflies were released. It was a nice gesture. I took a picture while they were being released.

A lot of the songs were from *Beggar's Banquet* and *Let it Bleed*, and during 'Midnight Rambler' a bunch of people sat a couple of yards in front of us got up and blocked our view. Everyone was trying to get them to sit down again. When it became apparent that they weren't going to, several people began shouting out to Mick, asking him to make them sit. They got Mick's attention, but instead of him shaming the standees he just shimmied his way to the other side of the stage as if to say, 'Hey, not my problem!' Fortunately, they did eventually sit down, but it was no thanks to Mick.

By the end of the concert, he had ditched the dress in favour of the pale mauve sleeveless t-shirt he was wearing underneath. He was full of energy and running and dancing all over the stage, but the concert itself was a bit ragged and I didn't think Mick Taylor looked very comfortable.

Then it was over, it had been an emotional and very tiring day but really was the end of an era. I still love the Stones and always will, but I never went to see them again.

ELAINE SPINKS

The memory of walking in Hyde Park towards the stage with thousands of other fans still brings goosebumps now. The atmosphere in the park that day was amazing – there was no trouble and my friend and I were right at the front side of stage. We saw Mick Jagger and Marianne Faithfull get out of a car backstage, and he waved. There was almost silence when they walked on stage, Mick with his white smock on and with the new guitarist Mick Taylor. Jagger spoke emotionally about the band's loss, then released some doves. You could have heard a pin drop, and then everyone cheered. What a day.

ANDY THOMPSON

I got to Hyde Park about a quarter to seven in the morning. It was a really hot day and we were possibly 80 yards off stage in the park for 6.45am. The Stones didn't come on until around 7pm, a long wait but well worth it. But they were absolutely rubbish that day. They were in an air-conditioned caravan because it was such a hot day and tuned all the guitars, and when they got on stage all the tuning went out. They weren't very good at all.

JILLY WILLIAMSON

It was a boiling hot day. Anticipating a huge crowd, myself and friends left Aylesbury on the first train, having been up all night to make quite sure we did so. We were at the park well before 8am and found a good position, not too near the stage on a slight rise to give us a good view. There were a few people around the stage and a couple of dog walkers. We slept. I still remember the amazement of waking in a crowd that stretched as far as the eye could see. It was a great show apart from the fainters from the heat, man-handled over heads to I don't know where. I didn't need the loo – which was just as well.

TED GARRATT

Family, a Leicester band, were on that bill as well and we wanted to see them so had planned on going anyway. But then Brian died and he'd been a hero to all of us, partly because he seemed to be the most musical of all the Stones. And because he said very little, even in interviews, you always wondered what made him tick. A car load of us went down and parked in an underground car park. We weren't part of the hysteria in that we couldn't have been much further away than anybody else in Hyde Park. We could hear the sound wafting over the breeze. It was a cultural as well as a musical thing to be there.

GUÐBJÖRG ÖGMUNDSDÓTTIR

Nothing could dampen my spirits that day. There was not a cloud in the sky. Within me I still felt the deep sorrow for Brian's sudden passing. But today was a celebration of his life and his music. A Danish friend from work was going with me. When we got out into the street outside the hospital where we had been working, we were filled with suspense and excitement. Almost immediately we noticed the headlines of the day on every other street corner. We stopped and bought some papers and saw pictures of people lying in sleeping bags in front of the enclosure in front of the stage. We had not realised people had started arriving at Hyde Park the evening before and the police, afraid they would have a riot on their hands, let them stay in the park throughout the night. This was unheard of – Hyde Park was always locked at night.

We hurried down to the Underground and made the short journey to the nearest station to where the concert was being held. The trains and sidewalks were filled with young people around our age and some a little older, a few a lot older. Everyone had long hair. We had never seen so many hippies walking along the streets, coming from all directions.

When we reached the area in front of the stage where people were already sitting and lazing in the sunshine, everyone was really cool and friendly. By this time my heart was beating so fast I thought I would have a nervous breakdown. I felt I needed to calm my nerves. To my surprise my friend pulled out a bottle of valium. She said she was going to take one and I took one too. We pulled out a sandwich to eat and a beer to drink with it and some of the people around us broke out in laughter and made some comments at us for being really uncool to have brought beer. We really felt embarrassed. Of course, we had smelled all the incense and joints in the air, and when a joint was handed our way we accepted and took a drag or two and gave out sandwiches or fruit in return. No one wanted our beer.

Everyone was really nice and friendly. It was a tremendous joy to be there among the crowd. I was amazed at the size of the crowd. It went on for as far as you could see. A few guys near us announced they had seen what they had come to see, and it was time to split – the Rolling Stones were sell-outs and not worth listening to anymore. The announcer explained Mick was going to read something for Brian and was asking all of us to be quiet while he did so. Then thousands of white butterflies would be released.

The Rolling Stones walked on stage and the roar of the crowd was unbelievable. They all looked so cool. Mick was wearing this incredible outfit. The next day the headline across the front page of one paper read, 'Where Did He Get That Frock?' He was all dressed in white and when he spoke everyone went quiet. It was the weirdest thing. But he didn't think the crowd was quiet enough. So he said, 'Are you going to shut up or not?' After that you could have heard a pin drop. Then he read Shelley's poem in remembrance of Brian. It was very beautiful. I could feel the pain stinging in my heart. I really felt like crying.

Right afterwards, brown cardboard boxes were brought out and thousands of beautiful white butterflies were released into the air. It looked so fitting and beautiful. I could feel my heart fill with joy. This was a moment in history that would not be forgotten.

The Stones were on stage for over an hour, performing lengthy versions of most of their songs. I felt empty inside after they left the stage. It almost seemed as if the sun had left the sky. Emotion was overcoming me and I suddenly felt all the anticipation, excitement and experience of the day overwhelm me. I staggered off the path and sat down under a great big tree. My friend followed me, and I told her I needed to take a moment to take all this in. Emotions absolutely overtook me, and I started shaking and crying. Tears were streaming down my face. Almost at the same time I started laughing uncontrollably. All the grief of Brian's passing that I had been holding in and the joy of seeing the Stones perform just had to come out. I felt unspeakably happy and sad at the same time. A couple of young guys came by and started asking what was wrong, but I couldn't talk. At last, one of them said he thought he knew what I was feeling, that I was crying for Brian and laughing due to the happiness of having just seen the Stones perform.

HELEN LOCK

The Hyde Park free concerts were big events and I was beyond excited to be going to the Stones show, dressed in my hippie finery. It had been so long since I'd seen them. We spent most of the day at the top of the incline, a pretty long way from the stage but with a perfect view, and with a good view of all the people in trees too.

When the Stones were about to come on, I wanted to get closer and wormed my way down toward the front. I was now right in the thick of things but couldn't see a thing. For one thing, the stage was very low. The show started and I was so excited to be hearing them again. The whole thing had the feel of a real occasion, especially with the introduction of Mick Taylor, and with everybody wondering how they would handle mentioning Brian's death.

I was overwhelmed and relieved because the music was so great – despite what naysayers have said in the years since, those of us down there in the crowd were having a blast – and a kind stranger lifted me up onto his shoulders so I could see Mick dancing in the white dress.

Later, all I caught were glimpses, but it was enough. It developed into a real party and the amazing thing is that this is despite the fact that so many of the songs were new to us (hence my problem with the set list). We didn't know 'Sympathy For The Devil', for example, but I remember everybody picking up cans and bottles and playing percussion on them, and some people actually brought tambourines and were playing them. I also saw butterflies flying around, but no dead ones – that was something I only learned about later. I had an amazing time and got home in time to watch the report of the event on the late-night news. Tired, but happy, as they say.

BOB LEE

We didn't see an awful lot because we were quite far back, but you could hear them clear enough. I remember walking round London and hearing this record coming out of somewhere and said, 'Listen to that – it's fantastic.' It was 'Honky Tonk Women', which came out that weekend. That was the first time I heard it, and it just blew me away.

THOMAS MARSCHIK

I had just finished my sophomore year in college. I missed meeting Keith Richards by 15 minutes as he came by the small hotel I was staying in near Paddington Station, about a ten-minute walk to Hyde Park. I slept in Hyde Park the night before the concert. There were perhaps a hundred of us in my area, where they were constructing the stage. Someone had a radio and I must have heard 'Honky Tonk Women' two dozen times that night – the song had been released that Friday. There was also an announcement that because we were orderly the police would not come in and evict us, as Hyde Park was always closed at night and no one was supposed to be there overnight. This caused someone to break apart a lawn chair and build a small fire. Luckily, we were not evicted.

If you watch the concert video on You Tube and freeze it seven seconds in, there is a guy sitting in the middle of the frame in a blue jacket, kind of by himself, from the back. That's me.

TRISH COLE

I went with my then boyfriend and three or four of his mates. We drove up from Ashtead in an open-top Land Rover and, if I remember correctly, we were able to drive into the park and leave the Land Rover quite close to the stage. I had long straight hair with a fringe then, and someone yelled, 'It's Marianne Faithfull!'

We were quite near the stage, where the ground began to rise away from the flat. People were mostly sitting and lying on the ground, with the odd person dancing. We were all very aware of the death of Brian Jones and I was interested to see how

Mick Taylor would fit in. I remember when the butterflies were released, although I believe that many of the butterflies died. I can't remember anything about the quality of the performance, but I liked Jagger's white 'dress'.

DANY MATER

I was living in Ilford. My friends and I were so excited about the concert. Then there was the shock of the awful shattering news of Brian's death, shortly after he was sacked from the band. The concert was first cancelled, adding to our grief, and then Mick Jagger announced the concert would finally be held in memory of Brian.

We went to Hyde Park hours before the concert was due to start and the weather was just glorious. There were hundreds of thousands of us in a peaceful gathering, between happiness and tears for Brian, and anxious to see Mick Taylor with the Stones. I had seen him before with John Mayall, and he was just an amazing musician. I was about halfway to the stage, near a tree which brought us some shelter from the blistering sun. Then they came on, and Mick read that beautiful poem by Shelley and released thousands of white butterflies (although I later heard they did not survive because they were not adapted to that environment).

Marsha Hunt was standing on the side of the stage at Hyde Park. What a beautiful lady. The whole event was emotion through and through, although it probably wasn't technically their best performance. They'd been away from the stage for quite a while, and they'd also been through rough times. Mick Taylor had only just joined and they had Brian's death to deal with on top of that. But there was a stunning 'Sympathy For The Devil', with wild African drums. I'll never forget that day.

DAVID ROBINSON

When we entered the park, Richie Havens was walking towards us, his guitar resting on his shoulder; it was quite surreal. There was a natural sort of amphitheatre, which overlooked the stage, and we found a spot on the bank approximately 50 yards from the stage. The crowd grew larger and larger as time went by. Eventually, there were around a quarter of a million people there.

There was a wide variety of mainly young people there, ranging from smartly dressed to Rocker types and flower-power types. I was 19 at the time and my friends were a year or two older. There was a fantastic party-type atmosphere. You knew what to expect from the Stones, and they didn't disappoint. It was different from the Blind Faith concert I'd seen earlier in the year in Hyde Park, where people were waiting to hear what they played. After the Stones concert, we hung around for a while then drifted back to the pub where our pal worked, before driving home.

DEN BOUNDY

Hyde Park was a wonderful experience – a lovely warm day with a lot of cool hippies around. There were various reports after that there were between 200,000 and 500,000 people there. My friend and I must have got there fairly early, as we got a good spot not too far from the stage. It was the only time I saw the Stones. I was quite shocked that Mick was wearing a white dress.

OLIVER BALL

I had never seen so many people together. We got there late and stood right at the back. Consequently, I didn't see much but it felt like you could hear them all over London. There was also something else everyone felt, as though we had been part of something special.

ROWAN WYMARK

I was 15. I'd just started doing drugs in a minor league way and was working my way toward dropping out of school. I wouldn't describe my then self as a hippie – I was a bit too young to have hit the full-blown Woodstock period. The Hyde Park concerts were pretty regular then. Blind Faith made their debut at one in June. I went to the Stones concert with a group of friends and a relatively new boyfriend. We missed all the warm-up bands but found a really good space to sit at which had a great view of the stage. I remember Mick in his light green dress, and the butterflies that were released becoming tangled in people's hair. The main thing I remember about the concert was the energy. Mick didn't let up and the whole stage crackled. It was as if sparks flew out and hit us all.

I knew at the time it was going to be a significant moment in history. I saw a Stones documentary not so long ago that included shots of the concert, and it was odd to realise that one of the 'blobs' that made up the huge audience was me.

JOHN PHILPOTT

My sidekick Chris Poole and I managed to convince the concert organisers, Blackhill Enterprises, that our local paper the *Rugby Advertiser* needed to cover the event. Our barefaced cheek paid off as, after a few calls, two sky blue tickets for the press enclosure arrived in the post. Chris was the main mover here, for he had struck up a friendship with concert promoter Sam Cutler, the man who not only oversaw that historic London gig but went on to become the Stones' chief road manager.

That Saturday Chris and I rose early and made our way to Rugby Midland Station only to find all the Euston-bound trains were full. Somehow, we managed to convince a guard our mission was urgent and he allowed us to ride in the mail carriage.

The sky was as blue as our tickets when we joined the crowds heading for Hyde Park. Being in the press enclosure meant we were in the company of the emerging rock aristocracy. In my case, that meant sitting next to pop starlet Marsha Hunt, a vision in white buckskins topped off with an Afro halo of hair. All manner of bands prepared the way for the Stones, most of them now little more than musical memories: Pete Brown's Battered Ornaments, Third Ear Band, Screw... Who knows what became of the musicians that helped to make history on that boiling hot day all those years ago?

A crowd of nearly half a million listened to them politely, if a little dutifully, then around mid-afternoon the Stones strode on stage. The footage has been played many times – Jagger in Greek soldier's ceremonial frock, Richards a living skull, and the rest looking rather bewildered. Introduced by Sam Cutler as 'The Greatest Rock 'n' Roll Band in the World', they were hopelessly out of tune, a vision of jaded rebellion that even then was showing signs of being very much part of a new Establishment.

They came and went. As Chris and I filed out of Hyde Park in the dusty heat of that July day, I reflected on the fact that my only sustenance all day had been a hamburger and Coke, both bought for what seemed like an extortionate amount. This had been the first big rock festival and the rip-off merchants had been more interested in LSD of a different kind! We caught the train back to Rugby, suspecting we had witnessed history in the making.

ALAN POWELL

We had to get the bus from Ellesmere Port in Cheshire. It was my first ever trip to London. Hyde Park was packed when we got there, full of strangely dressed people lying on the floor smoking long roll-ups. There was nothing like that in Ellesmere Port… and no free love either!

We climbed a tree but it didn't help so we sort of wove our way forward, stepping on the occasional ankle. The British Hell's Angels didn't look that tough, a bit like some of the hard knocks at home. We watched the exotic girls climbing up on the stage and sat by them as they played. 'Was that Marianne?' 'There's Suzy Creamcheese!' And we saw Keith with the Gibson V – so cool.

The press said they were out of tune, that Jagger had a dress on, that the butterflies they planned to release were already dead. But we loved them, and this was a rare chance to see them. They were getting so remote and untouchable. They'd been in the papers, acing jail. We bloody loved them – leave 'em alone!

10 JULY 1969

CHELTENHAM CEMETERY AND CREMATORIUM
CHELTENHAM
UK

"Please don't judge me too harshly"

BRIAN JONES

Brian Jones is laid to rest. His funeral is attended by Charlie Watts and Bill Wyman. Mick is away in Australia to film the movie *Ned Kelly*, in which he is to play the lead role.

12 SEPTEMBER 1969

OLYMPIC SOUND STUDIOS
CHURCH ROAD
BARNES
LONDON
UK

"We did the most brilliant stuff together (with Mick Taylor), some of the most brilliant stuff the Stones ever did. Everything was there in his playing – the melodic touch, a beautiful sustain and a way of reading a song"

KEITH RICHARDS

"There aren't many fixed plans at the moment. They want to do some playing in America in October, but there are problems. Certain cities still won't allow the Stones to play there, and it's hard enough to find a suitable place anyway. But they're all well pleased with playing publicly again, and they want to do more. Even though Mick's doing very well as a film actor, music is far and away the main thing. Everybody's playing is getting better, and they're really keen again. Everything's going very well indeed"

IAN STEWART, ROLLING STONES TOUR MANAGER

Mick Jagger returns from Australia to join the rest of the Stones, who have been recording material for *Let It Bleed.*

JOHN ELLIS, FAN

The music scene had changed since they went off the road in 1967. In 1968 and 1969, rock music had become popular. Cream, Hendrix and especially Led Zeppelin radically changed fans' expectations. The 1967 version of the Stones was quaint compared to the 1969 rock scene. For their 1969 tour, the Stones started using much louder amps, and with the addition of Mick Taylor, they had a bona fide soloist. However, new rock music was being released each week. Rock albums, a rarity in 1967, started picking up steam in 1968, and by 1969 rock music was no longer underground. It was the new music for a whole younger generation, many of whose first album was Led Zeppelin's first, released in early 1969.

14 SEPTEMBER 1969

"Our sort of scene is to have a really good time with the audience. It's always been the Stones' thing to get up on stage and kick the crap out of everything. We had three years of that before we made it, and we were only just getting it together when we became famous. We still had plenty to do on stage and I think we still have. That's why the tour should be such a groove for us

"Apart from people wanting to see us, we really need to do a tour, because we haven't played live for so long. A tour's the only thing that knocks you into shape. Especially now that we've got Mick Taylor in the band, we really need to go through the paces again to really get it back together… What decided us to get back into it was Hyde Park. It was such a unique feeling…"

KEITH RICHARDS

THE ROLLING STONES 1969 TOUR

The Rolling Stones announce to the press that they will tour the United States later in the fall.

November 8	The Forum, Los Angeles, California
November 9	Oakland Coliseum, Oakland, California
November 10	Sports Arena, San Diego, California
November 11	Coliseum, Phoenix, Arizona
November 13	Moody Coliseum, Dallas, Texas
November 14	Coliseum, Auburn University, Auburn, Alabama
November 15	University of Illinois, Champaign, Illinois
November 16	Chicago International Amphitheater, Chicago, Illinois
November 24	Olympia Stadium, Detroit, Michigan
November 25	The Spectrum, Philadelphia, Pennsylvania
November 26	Civic Center, Baltimore, Maryland
November 27 & 28	Madison Square Garden, New York
November 29	Boston Garden, Boston, Massachusetts
November 30	West Palm Beach Pop Festival, West Palm Beach, Florida

17 OCTOBER 1969

HEATHROW AIRPORT
LONDON
UK

The Rolling Stones fly to Los Angeles to prepare for their US tour.

17 OCTOBER – 2 NOVEMBER 1969

SUNSET SOUND RECORDING STUDIOS
6650 WEST SUNSET BOULEVARD
LOS ANGELES
CALIFORNIA

ELEKTRA SOUND RECORDERS
962 LA CIENEGA BOULEVARD
WEST HOLLYWOOD
CALIFORNIA

The Stones go into studios in Los Angeles to work on tracks for *Let It Bleed*, including 'Country Honk' and 'Gimme Shelter'.

28 OCTOBER - 1 NOVEMBER 1969

BASEMENT
STEPHEN STILLS HOUSE
3615 SHADY OAK ROAD
LAUREL CANYON
LOS ANGELES
CALIFORNIA

"Sharing a house with Mick, Keith and Mick Taylor sometimes felt like living with three English gentlemen in a sedate country hotel"

SAM CUTLER

"We did some rehearsals. We didn't do a lot. You know what the Stones are like. It was mostly party time"

BILL WYMAN

The Stones rehearse for the tour in Stephen Stills' basement.

2 - 5 NOVEMBER 1969

SOUND STAGE FOUR
WARNERS BROS
3400 WARNER BOULEVARD
BURBANK
CALIFORNIA

"Nobody told me what time"

BILL WYMAN

The Stones rehearse on the partially dismantled set for the movie *They Shoot Horses, Don't They?* Bill Wyman is absent.

27 OCTOBER 1969

BEVERLY WILSHIRE HOTEL
WILSHIRE BOULEVARD
BEVERLY HILLS
CALIFORNIA

"We aren't doing this tour for money, but because we want to play America and have a lot of fun. We're really not into that sort of economic scene. I mean, either you're gonna sing and all that crap or you're gonna be a fucking economist. We're sorry people can't afford to come. We don't know that this tour is more expensive. You'll have to tell us"

MICK JAGGER

JIM RISSMILLER, CONCERT ASSOCIATES (PROMOTER)

We're making money, sure, but we make a lot more with the Iron Butterfly in Anaheim. But the cost of the tickets? That's the Stones' responsibility. They set the prices, not us.

6 NOVEMBER 1969

MADISON SQUARE GARDEN
BOX OFFICE NEW YORK
NEW YORK

"What I hope the Stones do is turn the whole country on, do what the Mets did for New York, wake 'em up. And I think the Stones can do it. Mick Jagger is the greatest fucking performer in the whole fucking world"

BILL GRAHAM

6,000 people stand in line at the Madison Square Garden box office to buy Rolling Stones tickets when they go on sale. Both evening performances sell out.

7 NOVEMBER 1969

MOBY GYMNASIUM
COLORADO STATE UNIVERSITY
FORT COLLINS
COLORADO

"Backstage was like a case of beer and some potato chips"

JAMES PAGLIASOTTI

JAMES PAGLIASOTTI

They opened the tour in Fort Collins, Colorado, which at that time was a little town. It was where Colorado State University happened to be. And that date on the tour came about because the Stones had not planned to play Denver and Barry Fey, who was a pretty prominent promoter by that time (and eventually a partner of Bill Graham and others) was very persuasive and convinced them to do what they called 'a warm-up show'. I believe it was the smallest venue they played on that tour. It seated about 15 or 16,000 people. And that tour was the beginning of the really big shows. Bands had obviously toured before that, but that was the first time in my experience that a band was going out with an entourage to conquer the United States and did so very successfully – until Altamont, of course.

In 1969, if you look at any of the photographs from that tour, the thing that strikes me always is there was a change that took place between the '69 and '72 tours that the Stones exemplified. In '69, it was still pretty much face-to-face between the band and the audience. The stage was raised, obviously, but not very high, and actually there were people with their elbows on the stage while the Stones were performing. It was that intimate, and even though they were starting to play to much larger crowds, there was still that intimacy. That really changed in '72.

I went on five shows on the '69 tour. Backstage was like a case of beer and some potato chips or something. In 1972, backstage was catered meals and premium brands of liquor and French champagne. It was all done on Persian carpets and it was quite a difference. And I think we saw that in the music too.

THOMAS MACCLUSKEY, *ROCKY MOUNTAIN NEWS*

The Stones were the Stones. Unchanged. Undiminished. Unbeatable. Mixing their oldies (but goodies) with a number of newies (also goodies), they projected their internationally known sound and personal magnetism back to the far corners of the huge field house... And then there's Mick Jagger. Wow! Better than ever... He's much warmer. Less aloof. More talkative. More responsive to his devotees appreciation of him... Keith's blues playing was especially impressive on 'When The Train Left The Station' ('Love In Vain'). The coloured effects created by overhead and stage-wing lights as well as distant spotlights enhanced the performance considerably.

THE COLLEGIAN

$35,000 was paid to have the British rock band come and play a single concert for the University. This concert also marked the opening night of one of the band's many US tours.

According to archive staff, the opening acts were Terry Reid and BB King. One review of the show said that BB King stole the show while the Rolling Stones were only average. A different review praised the Stones and said that King and his band were too commercialised.

According to archive documents, the appearance of the Rolling Stones at CSU can be accredited to American rock concert promoter Barry Fey. Fey booked the band's tour before he was able to get a venue in Denver, all of which were booked at the time. As such, Fey decided to approach the program director at CSU about renting out Moby Gym. Not wanting to take any financial risks, CSU agreed as long as they received money from both rent and gate payment. The athletic department got $1,000 for rent and $5,000 from their cut of the gate receipts.

Fey received another bill following the performance from CSU, this time charging him $6,000 for the extensive clean-up and damage repair required as a result of the concert.

The Rolling Stones mandated that no photographs be taken of the event.

ERIN UDELL, *THE COLORADOAN*

Here's a full list of the damages left behind:

- 193 cigarette burn holes on basketball floor ($2,200)
- Burned tarp ($3,000)
- Damaged windows in north concourse ($262)
- Damaged glass in four entrance doors ($151)
- Two broken Kotex machines ($70)
- Damaged interior tile ($70)
- Damage to walls in men's restroom, requiring sanding and repainting ($28)
- Broken towel dispenser in men's restroom ($25)
- Damaged ceramic tiles in Portal D ($25)
- Trash pickup ($20)
- Burned carpet in Lettermen's Lounge ($15)
- Damaged door jam ($7.50)

8 NOVEMBER 1969

THE FORUM
INGLEWOOD
CALIFORNIA

"When I saw the full-page ad in the *Los Angeles Sunday Times*, I couldn't think of anything else the rest of that day but that I had to get tickets to see them"

ERNEST SALGADO

ERNEST SALGADO

I first discovered the Rolling Stones when I was about twelve years old. It was in the early 1960s, during the first British Invasion as we called it here in the US, when The Beatles reigned supreme and Beatlemania was all the rage. But by the end of 1964, right about the time when the Merseybeat pop explosion was waning, the Rolling Stones started to stand out for me, especially with their duo guitar-driven Chuck Berry-Bo Didley rhythm assault on the senses, and when it seemed everybody else was trying to be cute, clean cut and Beatle-like, with their moptops and matching suits.

Not only did the Stones seem a little less cute than the rest but they were tougher and more rebellious looking and their music – which was pretty much based on American black music – sounded tough too. Their toughness probably came from years of listening to and covering the Blues and Rhythm & Blues which came out of some of the toughest cities in America such as Memphis, Chicago and Detroit. That's about as tough and gritty as it gets, especially for a bunch of white boys from England, which was an inimitable dichotomy.

Not only did they embrace this music, they were immersed in it and got down with it, and by the time they had their biggest number one, the 1965 original composition '(I Can't Get No) Satisfaction', they were already considered by many to be one of the era's top white R&B/Blues bands on both sides of the pond.

The very first album I ever bought by them was *Out Of Our Heads* in 1966, when I was around 15 years old. I remember buying it with left over lunch money that I'd save all week. For a time, when it was the one and only album that I owned, I would listen to that album every day after I got home from school, over and over multiple times.

By 1969, I had most of the albums they had put out, but it wasn't until *Beggars Banquet* and especially *Let It Bleed* that they truly established themselves with their very own brand and original sound, thanks in part to Keith's guitar playing and composing in open G tuning. When *Let It Bleed* came out, I and a couple of my bandmates kept trying to figure out how Keith was able to get that sound on his guitar. I remember saying to one of them that the only way to play those full-sounding chords with all the seventh notes was to have seven fingers instead of five!

Of course, that was because we were trying to figure it out on a standard guitar with a classic A-440 tuning, but even before Keith started to play and write songs in that tuning, the guitar interplay between him and Brian was one of the things about that band I always liked and enjoyed, and with ex-John Mayall and the

Bluesbreakers' guitarist Mick Taylor taking Brian's place after he left the band, it promised to be even more interesting.

When I saw the full-page ad in the *Los Angeles Sunday Times* during the summer of 1969 that read, 'For the first time in three years, welcome back to the US the Rolling Stones,' I couldn't think of anything else the rest of that day but that I had to get tickets to see them.

The day they went on sale, me and the guys I was in a band with cut school and went down to Wallich's Music City, which used to be on the corner of Sunset Boulevard and Vine Street in Hollywood, California to buy our tickets. They were for the first of two shows that evening, at 7pm on Saturday, November 8 1969 at the Fabulous Forum in Inglewood, California. The price per ticket started at $4.50 followed by $5.50, $6.50 and $7.50. We bought the $6.50 ones. The second show was to follow at 11pm.

The day of the concert we got there early. The show started at least an hour late, which made the wait seem even longer. I remember we had pretty good seats, on the first row of the upper loge and in a section that was left of the stage at about a 30 to 45-degree angle from its centre. The opening act was Terry Reid, who I didn't know much about. I remember very little of what he played. But BB King was fantastic with his whole blues ensemble, and so were The Ike and Tina Turner Revue.

When the Stones finally came on and hit the stage, it must have been around 10.30pm and they were introduced by their road manager, who was saying over the PA, 'Are you ready? Is everybody ready? After three years, the Rolling Stones! The Rolling Stones!'

Jagger appeared with an Uncle Sam top hat and the Omega sign on his t-shirt and with the first guitar chords of 'Jumpin' Jack Flash', the whole 18,000-strong arena crowd went into one big roar of cheering fans. It was magical seeing all of them in the flesh for the first time, standing there playing in front of that wall of Ampeg amps.

When the song finished, Jagger joked with the audience with that now famous line about his trousers, and then they went straight into Chuck Berry mode with 'Carol', followed by a groovy rocking rendition of 'Sympathy For The Devil', which vamped out during its coda with one of the most fiery dual lead guitar exchanges between Taylor and Richards ever. It was followed by another *Beggar's Banquet* gem, 'Stray Cat Blues', and then the lights went down and Jagger and Richards sat for a bluesy folk rendition of 'Prodigal Son' and 'You Gotta Move'. Next, with the full band, was 'Love In Vain' which showcased a beautifully played slide guitar by Mick

Taylor, followed by 'I'm Free' and 'Under My Thumb'.

'Midnight Rambler' was a total show stopper and to this day I still believe that that evening's live version was better than the version that is on the studio album. Jagger's theatrics, with his belt hitting the stage at the strike of each chord in coordination with the lights in the song's mid-section, along with his vocal and visual interpretation, were top-notch.

By the time they ripped right into 'Live With Me' everyone was out of their seat and up on their feet. We had left our seats to try to get as close as possible, and managed to get to the end of the lower loge, which was the last section before you reached the floor. We stood on a ledge that was almost at eye level with the stage and stayed there through 'Little Queenie', '(I Can't Get No) Satisfaction', 'Honky Tonk Women' and 'Street Fighting Man', which ended the show.

I remember it was way past midnight and we all had to exit through one side of the Forum, so that all the poor devils who had been waiting out in the cold for three hours could finally come in for the later show. I remember thinking to myself that they were probably going to end up having to stay there until 5am. Which was crazy, because many of them already looked like they were ready for bed.

The Stones have always been a great band to watch at any age throughout the years. But I can say with all certainty that being able to witness them play live all those years ago when they were in their mid-twenties was entirely something else. Their youthfulness was beautiful, and their rebelliousness and rock 'n' roll fury were both intoxicating and contagious.

I'm glad I was there.

HARVEY KUBERNIK

I saw two shows by the Stones in 1969 at the Forum in Inglewood. My mind was blown but I realised I could never really be in a band like them. I was happy to dig the sound and the pound.

MICHAEL IHDE

I've seen the Stones 15 times, and that first time in 1969 still stands out as one of those events that you'll probably never ever see again at any concert.

I remember when 'Satisfaction' came out. A group of us were playing a street baseball game and this kid came out of his house and said, 'You guys have got to hear this 45 I have.' We went into his house and we stayed there for about 45 minutes listening to 'Satisfaction' until we had all the lyrics to the song down. I just couldn't get enough. I bought the first two or three albums that had already come out, and from '65 onwards I purchased every album they ever made.

'69 was the first time I saw them live. I was 20. The *LA Times* had a rock critic called Robert Hilburn. They gave him two or three columns a week to write about what was going on with rock and roll here and this guy was like a kind of preacher. He controlled and documented everything that was going on regarding pop music in Southern California, and I was a fanatical follower of his.

I basically was buying season tickets to all the venues here – the Greek Theater in LA, the Universal Amphitheater in LA. You could get season tickets to see a minimum of six concerts for about $7 a show there. And from then until all the way through to about 2010, I had a 40-year run where I had season tickets to those two venues. Plus, I would occasionally go to the LA Coliseum to see the Stones in front of 80,000 or 90,000 people, and the Rose Bowl in Pasadena, where big concerts were also held.

To get tickets in '69, I just went to Ticketmaster. I bought four tickets, for my girlfriend and I and for my best friend and his girlfriend. There were two concerts scheduled for that night at the Forum. The first one was to have started at seven o'clock and the second show at eleven. We had tickets for the first show.

But I don't know what happened when they did the scheduling, because the LA Kings ice hockey team had an afternoon hockey game scheduled for one o'clock that day. So a hockey game was going to be followed immediately by a concert that was supposedly starting two hours afterwards. And there was absolutely no way they could get things set up in time.

So as the crowd for the seven o'clock concert started to arrive, we were told to wait outside for about a half hour. And then at 7.30pm, they started letting people in. And we went in and saw that they were still trying to put the stage and the lights up. We had assigned seats, up in the colonnade and looking straight down on the stage. We sat around there for about two and a half hours waiting for the stage to be set up.

The seven o'clock show started at 9.30pm. The line-up was Terry Reid, BB King, Ike and Tina Turner, and then the Stones. Terry Reid came out and played about a 15-minute set, and there was really no break before BB King came out and played a 30-minute set. And then the Ike and Tina Turner Revue came on and played a 35 to 40-minute set.

The Stones came on at about 11.10pm or 11.15pm. They did their full 90-minute set, somewhere about 14, 15, 16 songs. They had just put out *Beggar's Banquet* and they were starting to airplay *Let It Bleed*, so even though there were a couple of oldies, most of the show was tracks from *Beggar's Banquet* and *Let It Bleed*. And obviously the place went nuts.

If you play *Get Your Ya-Ya's Out*, that's the kind of sound it was. I still play *Ya-Ya's* all the time. Side two of that album is absolutely killer. They did 'Jumpin' Jack Flash' and they did a couple of slow songs off that album. For the most part, that album as a live album symbolises how they sounded at the concert that I went to.

Two or three of them were the best rock and roll shows I've ever seen. And I've probably been to hundreds of concerts. I had season tickets for just about everything. And I've seen all those big 60s groups. From an experience perspective the Forum concert was a once-in-a-lifetime experience. But from a sound perspective, I've seen them at Anaheim Stadium in a big stadium setting, I've seen them at Dodger Stadium and I've seen them at the Hollywood Bowl and they were all good shows. But the problem is when you've got 50,000, 60,000 people in there, it's just not quite the same as the intimate setting of about 18,000 to 20,000.

I saw them in '72 when Stevie Wonder opened up for them. They did a good show but it just didn't have the vibe that the Forum did. People ask me all the time, 'Were you at one of those shows?', and when I tell them they just kind of shake their heads and laugh.

18,000 people walked out into the Forum parking lot at 12.30am and there were 18,000 people out there waiting to get in for the eleven o'clock show. You saw 18,000 people amongst all these parked cars trying to get into the second show. They had to clean the place up before they let the other 18,000 come in for the second show. It was a real fiasco. And I believe they didn't start that second show around 2.45am or three o'clock in the morning and let them out at 6am.

LISA HILL

It was my very first Stones concert and I was 16 years old. I still have the programme (they had beautiful programmes in those days) and it was the most amazing experience of my young life. I had been a fan since I heard 'Tell Me' when I was ten years old, but this was the first really major concert I had ever been to and my first Stones concert. It was quite the happening. In those days you knew so many people there. You'd be walking in and seeing kids you went to school with or worked with. (I was working at 16.) You dressed up in cool concert clothes with a rock and roll vibe… this was Los Angeles, mind you. I don't remember seeing BB or Terry Reid but Ike and Tina were an amazing opening act. Even so I was *dying* for the Stones to come out. They were late (of course).

The song that's burned into my memory is 'Midnight Rambler'. It was so intense and sexually charged. Audiences were so young then and everybody was going nuts. When we left there was a whole new audience waiting (and waiting and waiting) to see the second show. They already looked pretty spent. I felt bad for them.

AUGGIE BICKER

The Los Angeles Lakers basketball team played at the Forum. Somehow, the powers-that-be messed up and booked the tour in for two concerts on the same night, only to discover there was a basketball game scheduled for that night too. That set the first gig back to just about when the second one, the show I attended, was originally scheduled to start. I'd heard the news on the radio but was already heading that way, so we went up to a friend's house in Westwood, drank wine and smoked dope until it was time to head to the Forum. It turned out that the second show didn't start until near midnight. It was a hoot!

MIKE ARENAS

I first heard the Rolling Stones in 1963 on a local station called KRLA Radio. It was a love 'at first sight', if you pardon the expression. I listened to the music and their albums as soon as they were released. I became a fan when I was in junior high. My brother bought me the Stones' latest album for Christmas and he continued to give me their latest release every Christmas from that day forward.

In 1969, I heard they were going to be at the Forum in Inglewood. My dad would not let me go to concerts before that, because he felt that it was full of sinners and lowlifes. I went to Ticketron to buy a ticket, but their allotted supply ran out. I was panicking and the fellow at Ticketron called me back and said, 'Hey look, why don't you take this number, give it a shot and call the Forum ticket office?'

As soon as I got home, I called the ticket office and I got a young man who was from the ticket dispersal office. He was very young sounding but he was really helpful. When I told him my situation he said, 'How many tickets would you like?'

I told him I'd like three. He held the call for a second and went to talk to someone. He came back and said, 'Can you use Western Union to send some money this way and we will see what we can do.' I was desperate so I said sure.

'Send me $30 and that's three tickets. And I'll make sure they're in a good spot.' It was too easy, and I was really nervous when the tickets didn't immediately arrive. But about a week before the concert, they finally did so I invited my brother and my cousin Steve to go with me. My brother offered to drive.

We had tickets for the nine o'clock show, which was the second show of the two that were being brought to LA area. We arrived at the car park to find that people who'd gone for the first concert were still there. And we found out later that people who had attended the hockey game were also still parked there. So there was no parking!

They directed us back to another street and then directed us into a driveway which led into a cemetery! We parked the car and as my brother got out, he said, 'Who is Betty Wagner?' We were parked on her grave.

We walked through Hollywood Park to the Forum and at nine o'clock, when our show was supposed to start, the hockey game was just ending. They laid a plywood floor over the ice and because the ice was condensating the 9 o'clock show didn't start until 11 o'clock. We had to find something to do for a few hours until our show started.

There was a liquor store close to the Forum and we went there to get something to eat or drink. The place was totally wiped out of food or any treats because of the long wait. All they had left was milk and beef jerky.

We finally got into the show at 2.30am. Our seats were incredible – stage high and maybe ten rows out on the first level. It was a perfect view. We'd had a couple of beers on the way there but when we got into the auditorium, we got what they called a contact high.

The two opening acts were BB King and Ike and Tina Turner. What a start!

There was a young lady next to me who I talked to a little bit when the concert started. She continually put her fingers into my mouth or around my lips. She was rubbing small pieces of plastic that were dipped in LSD all over my mouth so I got a slight high, but nothing really serious. I finally got angry and told her to stop.

The Stones started at 4.30am and it was an incredible show. I was so happy that I went. By the time we got out of the concert, it was very late. On the drive home the sun was coming up. When we got home, my parents thought we were up early to go to church with them. My brother said, 'No, we just got home – we're going to bed!'

I've been a fan since 1963 but I stopped going to their concerts after the 1975 show at the Forum because they had announced they were going to do outdoor stadium concerts and I really hate those. I didn't return to see the Stones live until 2015 and I am really sorry I waited so long. But you can't cry over spilled beer.

My brother was a good man and I miss him dearly.

TOM MCCARTER

I was only interested in rock. I wasn't really aware of soul, R&B or blues music, although I knew the names Ike and Tina Turner and BB King. In the middle of one of the songs that Tina was singing, which was very lascivious, she started licking the microphone. Later I bought the *Ya-Ya's* box set that included the BB King and the Ike and Tina Turner sets from the New York show (plus songs the Stone did that were left off the original album) and I had hoped that she would be licking the microphone there as well, but she did not.

BB King and Ike and Tina Turner both turned in spirited sets which impressed me. Terri Reid did not impress, though I have heard he was an excellent guitar player. It seemed like he was out of his league. I have read later that they had wanted Chuck Berry to be opening along with Ike and Tina Turner and BB King: the cream of blues, R&B and rock and then the Stones would come on and put it all together. That would've been awesome.

The Stones really rocked the house and they had all of their best tunes at that point. The *Ya-Ya's* album captures their energy and delivery perfectly. That said, I can't remember anything that really grabbed me during their set. No extended solo from Keith or whatever. Still, in my book that was the Stones at the top of their game. Subsequent albums disappointed. I did go to see them once again. It was in Hawaii in Honolulu and I just happened to be in town and managed to get a ticket. ZZ Top opened. I had never heard them before. They blew me away. The Stones really had to crank it up when they came on after them.

TOM DONAHUE, *CASH BOX*

The tour started at The Forum in Los Angeles on November 8 after the Stones had been in town for a couple of weeks of rehearsals and hanging out. The 18,000-seat house was sold out for both shows at a top ticket price of $12.50, though the advertised top was $7.50 with the first twenty rows of $12.50 tickets being reserved for the 'in' crowd. A great number of equipment problems, etc., delayed the start of both shows. The first show never quite got it together but the second was so good that the fans hardly noticed that it didn't end until 5.30am.

ROLLING STONE MAGAZINE

Tickets in Los Angeles sold out in eight hours, a total of 36,000 seats for two shows. About three hundred people waited overnight in front of the box office to get the first seats.

At first the Stones were criticised for asking so much money that the concert promoters apparently felt it was necessary to charge as much as $7.50 a ticket. Then it was discovered $7.50 wasn't even the top price – that the promoters, radio station KRLA and Concert Associates had held back the first twenty rows of seats for 'friends' in the industry, from whom they were asking $12.50 a ticket.

This meant that so long as the concerts' top price was being advertised as $7.50, kids who bought the expensive tickets assumed they were buying seats fairly close to the stage. November 8, they wouldn't even be within screaming distance.

IAN DOVE, *RECORD MIRROR*

The opening concert was delayed because of a double booking at the venue – the Stones and their fans clashed with the local ice hockey team. This meant that the opening concert started at midnight and meant that the second house crowd, plus their cars (LA is *the* automobile city of the world) were all yelling and honking outside the stadium.

So the next show started in the early, early hours and poor Terry Reid, who opened the first concert, was yanked off the bill because of time... It was 4am when Jagger and company mounted the stage before the 17,500 wound-up fans. The Stones proceeded to wind everyone up even further during their two-hour stint as they paraded their material. Titles like 'Satisfaction' and 'Honky Tonk Women' drew the biggest ovations but it was the climatic 'Street Fighting Man' that really pushed over the communication barriers.

There was Mick Jagger crawling around the stage all whipped up with emotion, whipping the stage with his trouser belt. There were 17,500 fans on their collective feet, their collective fists outstretched and clenched. Youth Power. For the Stones' management it was an anxious time. The security guards did not receive any overtime and so left stage and group unguarded. No matter though, the Stones finished. They were hustled into waiting limousines, and the crowd left.

ANN MOSES, *NEW MUSICAL EXPRESS*

At the Rolling Stones' first US concert in three years Mick Jagger strutted out on stage yelling, 'Has it really been three years?' and everybody agreed that it certainly didn't seem like it. Mick bounced through the show wearing a black outfit with a jaunty US stars and stripes hat. Their first number? 'Jumpin' Jack Flash' naturally!

Chuck Berry's 'Oh Carol' followed with piano accompaniment by the mysterious Stu, conspicuous in an all-white tuxedo. Keith looked rumpled and uncombed, but never sounded better! Boyish Mick Taylor and sombre Bill Wyman added intricate and inventive guitar work into the solid Stones' repertoire.

Charlie Watts, looking nobly bored as ever, more than adequately carried through on drumming, all the time appearing like a California surfer in his knit striped t-shirt. No one could see, but chances are he was wearing tennis shoes!

The Stones stayed on stage well over an hour and a quarter for their first show and an hour and three-quarters for their second show, which didn't get out until 5.15 am.

They performed several brand new songs and a mixture of old ones, like 'Stray Cat Blues', 'Prodigal Son' and 'Honky Tonk Woman'.

'Since you've been so good, we're gonna sit down and play for you...' Mick told the audience... and they did. Keith and Mick squatted on chairs, while Keith plucked out a down-home-blues number (which they never identified, but it's on the new album). Mick sang a nice, simple folksy blues line at his elbow.

'Midnight Rambler', another new Stones number, was an audience favourite and kept girls gyrating in the aisles of the 18,000-seater Forum auditorium. Half way through, Mick was on his knees, whacking his belt against the stage and then twirling it around his head, whispering 'don't do that...' into the microphone.

At the late show, after they had performed for an hour and 15 minutes, Mick told the audience, 'It's been three years and we're really having fun. If it's okay, we'd like to play a little longer for you.'

Well, the understatement of the year was that the audience thought it was okay, and they let Mick know!

The crowd went wild throughout the show, but not like three years ago. The audience, heavily male attended, wasn't the same hero worshipping crowd that showed up last time around. Perhaps because the ticket prices were $4.50 to $7.50 (and $12.50 for the first 20 rows!), the audience was older and more sophisticated.

The ravers who once yelled, 'Mick... Mick... we love you!' were notably absent. The scene has switched from personality worship to music appreciation and the Stones were glad!

They couldn't forget it – and they didn't. 'Satisfaction', complete with red stage light, nearly closed the show. 'Street Fighting Man' was their last rousing number – and they exited while the crowd screamed and pushed toward the stage. But no one grabbed for the Stones. They walked through the jubilant crowd in complete safety. Tearing at their clothes was for three years ago – remember?

9 NOVEMBER 1969

OAKLAND-ALAMEDA COUNTY COLISEUM ARENA
OAKLAND
CALIFORNIA

"We're really pleased to be back here. Really! No bullshit... We know it's a bit late, but we really hope you don't mind if we stay"

MICK JAGGER

JOE PRUSS

It was typical for teenagers from that era to like either the 'good boy' Beatles or the 'bad boy' Rolling Stones. Cheryl was a Rolling Stones fan and I was a Beatles fan. I met my wife in the summer of 1969. We were both 18 years old. We met at Bass Lake, California, when my friends and I arrived to a full campground. We drove through and found a late-night campfire, with like-minded teenagers, who invited us to join them. I was attracted to this beautiful blonde girl, named Cheryl. We've been together now for 56 years.

Cheryl was raised in Seattle, Washington, the home of country singer Lorreta Lynn, and her parents listened to the country radio stations playing Lorreta Lynn, Hank Williams, Johnny Cash and Patsy Cline. My childhood home was filled with the sounds of Frank Sinatra, Judy Garland and Julie London and Broadway musicals such as *Porgy And Bess*, *West Side Story* and *Oklahoma*.

My parents moved to Livermore when I was in the eleventh grade. I was the singer in a garage band in high school called The Jam and Jelly Counterplot. We played a few high school parties, not because we were good but more likely because our drummer was Miss Livermore, Sharon Gruhlke. (Sharon later married the President of the Oakland Chapter of the Hell's Angels, Sonny Barger. Some sort of synchronicity there?)

We had a few Rolling Stones hits in our repertoire; 'Satisfaction', 'The Last Time', 'Play With Fire' and 'Get Off My Cloud'. Cheryl had been a member of the Rolling Stones Fan Club since Junior High School and expanded my interest in them over the summer of '69.

Prior to Cheryl and I meeting, Cheryl was already expanding her musical interests to include the new cosmic country music coming out in 1969 including the Flying Burrito Brothers with Gram Parsons, Poco, and Crosby Stills Nash and Young.

We were fans of the newly published *Rolling Stone* magazine and somehow bought or borrowed every issue that summer of '69. In it, Cheryl saw the announcement of a Rolling Stones tour kicking off in the fall with the Oakland Coliseum show on November 9th. Our 'go to' place to buy tickets to concerts was a small record store next to the Livermore Theater, where Mike would know our interests and save tickets for us until we could get enough cash to purchase them.

Near the end of the summer of 1969, with Cheryl and I being together for a few months, Mike scored us two seventh row tickets for $7.00 each (no service charge) to the Rolling Stones' first show: the 6.30pm show at the Oakland Coliseum.

We had both attended rock and roll shows as teenagers and we prepared by dressing in the latest fashion, and Cheryl even curled her hair for the occasion. We arrived early and got high before entering the Oakland Coliseum for the 6.30pm start. The line-up opened with Terry Reid, followed by BB King and then Ike and Tina Turner. We were unfamiliar with these acts but clearly remember Tina Turner and her Ikettes dancing and doing 'Proud Mary'. The opening acts were complemented by production we hadn't experienced at prior rock shows, with the sound and lights and the dance routines all new for us.

Two hours in, the anticipation of the headlining Rolling Stones was hitting the ceiling of the Coliseum. When, around 8pm, the voice of Sam Cutler announced, 'Ladies and gentlemen, the Rolling Stones,' everyone stood up and stayed standing for the entire one and a half hour set.

This was the first Rolling Stones tour with their new guitarist, Mick Taylor, who replaced Brian Jones in June of 1969. Similar to the Yardbirds touring without Jeff Beck (replaced by Jimmy Page), the audience was apprehensive about this new guy.

The setlist included 'Jumpin' Jack Flash', 'Carol', 'Sympathy For The Devil', 'Stray Cat Blues', 'Prodigal Son', 'You Gotta Move', 'Love In Vain', 'I'm Free', 'Under My Thumb', 'Midnight Rambler', 'Live With Me', 'Gimme Shelter', 'Little Queenie', '(I Can't Get No) Satisfaction', 'Honky Tonk Women' and 'Street Fighting Man'.

I remember Keith looking out of it when he and Mick sat on chairs solo and did 'Prodigal Son' and 'You Gotta Move'. Despite his apparent condition the sound of his solo acoustic guitar filled the Coliseum without missing a note.

Midway during the set, Mick encouraged the audience to get closer to the stage. Since we were in the seventh row and near the aisle, we were the first to reach the stage. Bill Graham was the promoter and at that time took a hands on approach to his shows. Cheryl and I clearly remember Bill Graham telling fans to return to their seats or the show would stop. Since we were in front, Bill Graham put his hands on my back and pushed me back down the aisle.

The show ran long and ended with 'Street Fighting Man' around 9.30pm, the time the second show of the evening was supposed to start. We were the last to exit the venue and successfully made the one-hour drive home to Livermore, both agreeing that this was the greatest show of our lives with the world's greatest rock and roll band!

BUCK LACEY

When I was 12 years old and living on the peninsula, south of San Francisco, I had some friends – neighbours – and Durkin was their name. They had a playroom downstairs and one of them had discovered a radio station in Oakland with the call letters KWBR. A couple of guys out of New York had moved out here and started this radio station that was all rhythm and blues. And that was my first really big epiphany. I wanted to play music and wanted to be involved in it. Before that, it was all my mother and father's 78s, the big bands and things like that, which I really loved. That was really my first introduction to popular music and show tunes, etc.

As a family we moved around a lot, but mainly in Northern California. I was at a local Dairy Queen, getting a milkshake, and they had a little tiny speaker up above the window. All of a sudden, they put on 'Roll Over Beethoven' and I said, 'Oh my God, what's this? What's going on here?' And so then it was Chuck Berry, it was Little Richard and Fats Domino and, out of San Francisco, The Coasters. It was coming on pretty strong in the Bay Area at that time.

At first, I really wasn't a big Elvis fan, but that changed pretty quick; Elvis and Gene Vincent and the Bluecaps, the rockabilly era was my next phase. And then when I was in high school in Sacramento, from '57 to '61, it was 'the folk scare of the sixties' and the Kingston Trio, and the groups where they had 17 guitars on stage and stuff like that. I had a folk singing group in high school and we did little gigs at pancake breakfasts, things like that. And the women's movement was starting. The girls that I was hanging out with in high school seemed a lot smarter than the boys. Then in '61 I graduated, and we moved back to San Francisco.

I was introduced to the Stones' early work when they were basically just a blues cover band and that really opened my eyes. Nobody thought they would last but I knew that these guys were both going to last and that they were going to really leave their mark on the music business.

In 1969 the Rolling Stones announced a US tour. I was working in a restaurant in Sausalito, California called The Trident. It was run by a couple of guys from New York who had had a pretty big folk club there. They had this vision of opening a restaurant right on the bay in Sausalito that would attract our generation. It had lots of plants around, and psychedelic murals on the ceiling and the walls. And it became very, very popular with everybody, including Bill Graham.

I had been working there for just a little bit and I remember coming in one day – I didn't have a shift or anything like that – and everybody was very excited. And I said, 'What's going on?' And they said, 'Well, Bill Graham stopped by and dropped off a bunch of tickets for the Rolling Stones concert.'

I said, 'Well, are there any left?' And it was, I swear to God, ten dollars. It was at the newly erected, newly-built Oakland Coliseum and indoors.

I said, 'Are there gonna be opening acts?' And they said, 'Yeah, it's gonna be Terry Reid and BB King and Ike and Tina Turner.' I said, 'Count me in,' and I laid down my ten bucks and got in the car and we all went over there.

I was in the tenth or eleventh row. There was a guy jumping up and down, screaming. He was just this kid and this was the first time he'd heard anything like that and he was just screaming, 'Rolling Stones, music, Rolling, Rolling Stones, music.'

Somebody had brought a jug of grape Kool-Aid or grape juice or something like that with a little mescaline in it so we were all… not really high, but pretty mellow. That kind of added to the thing. It was the *Let It Bleed* tour, and that's one of their best albums as far as I'm concerned. It was just mind-blowing.

But the show was terrific. I haven't seen a show like it since. Terry Reid opened, and I always did like Terry Reid. And then it was BB, and I've always been a big BB King fan, and Ike and Tina Turner. And so by the time the Stones got there, everybody was just super primed for it.

'68, '69 was so tumultuous in our country. Everything was changing. People were getting killed, assassinations, Kent State, all of that stuff. The *Let It Bleed* album was the perfect analogy for that. Just the title alone was a nod to it. I remember the performance of 'Midnight Rambler' more than anything else from that concert.

GALLIVAN BURWELL

When the Rolling Stones show in Oakland was announced it was a big deal. Their previous tours hadn't caused much of a stir in the US, but by '69 they were an event. I'd been a fan since I first heard 'Not Fade Away' on AM radio, and their first album was a birthday gift in '64, when I turned 14. I owned every album, and dragged them – and all The Beatles, Dylan, Kinks, Donovan, Byrds, etc. – with me in a huge heavy box of vinyl and my one-piece stereo when I took a Trailways bus to Berkeley in June of '68, three days after graduating high school in Miami.

Up to the '69 tour I'd only been to two large auditorium-size shows, both in Miami: The Dave Clark 5 in December of '65 (they were terrific), and Bob Dylan three months later (the night that pretty much everybody in Miami's 'underground' scene showed up in the same place at the same time and the whole game changed). By spring of '67 there were a few clubs that booked major(ish) acts. I saw Spirit at The World, and the Mothers, the Dead, Country Joe and Cream at a psychedelic former bowling alley called Thee Image.

Once I got to the Bay Area, music was much more accessible, though I was pretty broke, so I hitched across the Bay to see bands in Golden Gate Park, and the occasional three-dollar Sunday night show at The Carousel/Fillmore West, or Family Dog on the Great Highway. But these were all small-venue shows, and the feeling at them was communal, including the audience relationship with the musicians. Weren't we all just part of the same community, them and us?

But the Stones were a whole other thing, and the show at the Coliseum Arena was the largest venue Bill Graham had booked. The buzz was on. *Let It Bleed* had been living on the stereo in the communal apartment I lived in since it came out. KSAN and KMPX played it nearly constantly. With The Beatles off the road, the Stones were as big it gets.

In those days I hung out on Telegraph Avenue ('The Ave') a lot, sold *Berkeley Barbs* on the corner on Fridays, sold bread and cheese from a cart at the entrance to Sproul Plaza a few days a week, and played guitar and sang my original songs at the occasional basket house gig to get by. Sometimes friends would come out from the East Coast and I'd middle-man acid or weed to them. I had a cute girlfriend I'd met on Telegraph (who later married Country Joe) and we took *lots* of psychedelics. I was 18.

One of the cats I knew on The Ave was a guy who worked for the Graham organisation called Mickey Mouse, and I bought two tickets for the early show from him. I think it was 15 bucks for both, maybe slightly less, certainly not more. When we arrived at the show we found our seats on the floor, about a quarter of the way back, very well situated.

There wasn't much in the way of ambience being offered. The seats were standard-issue metal cafeteria chairs. The stage set-up was also standard issue, just amps and drums set up in front of a theatre curtain on a stage not even waist-high off the ground. Can you imagine such a thing today?

Nobody was there to see the opening acts. BB King's was the standout for me. I'd never even heard of Terry Reid (and rightly so). Ike and Tina were their usual histrionic selves.

Then the Stones equipment was hauled onstage by a few burly roadies. No banks of amps, not much more than you'd see onstage at the Fillmore. Just a rock and roll band doing a gig.

The thing that struck me most of all was Keith just strolling out, rooster-hair skinny with a sash around his waist, carrying a see-through Dan Armstrong guitar. When he plugged it in it crackled, and he fooled around with it for a couple minutes, increasingly frustrated. A roadie walked out and changed out the cord, which didn't help. Keith took the guitar off his shoulders and threw it onto the floor. Out came a

Les Paul that sounded great, and plenty loud. Keith played a few chords, the house lights went down and the rest of the band took the stage to a roaring welcome.

There were no Beatlemania screams like the deafening row I'd experienced at the DC5 show. This was a hip, Bay Area audience. We weren't part of the same community as the Stones, but we were still cool.

The set was pretty much what you hear on the *Ya-Ya's* album from later in the tour, right down to the 'think I broke a button on my trousers' bit from Mick in his Uncle Sam hat and Leo astrological symbol shirt. It was fabulous, over too soon and out into the Oakland night we went to cadge a ride back to Berkeley.

MIKE WISEMAN

I went with my girlfriend, who is now my wife, and we saw them with Ike and Tina Turner. When Mick asked the stage crew to turn the lights on in the hall and invited the crowd to come down to the front of the stage, hundreds of people mobbed the stage and started jumping up on it and had to be taken off by security guards. There was a fight between Bill Graham and the Stones road manager on stage. Bay Area audiences who were fans of the Stones didn't usually act like this. They usually showed up at the Fillmore and Winterland and were very calm listeners. They just didn't get all excited like the teeny boppers did. When Mick invited them to come down front, all that changed. Little did we know that this would be a portent of things to come.

RANDY STANLEY

Visiting my cousins' house in the middle of 1965, they were playing music that was definitely not The Beatles. It was *The Rolling Stones, Now!* and much rougher and raw than The Beatles. For me it was like, 'Holy crap, I've got to have more of this.' From then on, it was the Stones only for me. In '66 I saw them for the first time at the Cow Palace in Daly City, just south of San Francisco. I was 13.

I saw them again in '69 at the Oakland Arena. I was 17 and went with my aunt, a friend and my first girlfriend (we're still friends). BB King and Ike and Tina Turner opened. The audience had changed in those three years. There were no more screaming girls, just people enjoying the music. And they played for an hour as opposed to the half hour I'd seen them do in '66. I remember 'Midnight Rambler', with Mick on his knees slapping the stage with his belt in time with Charlie hitting the drums. It may be my favourite song to see live although that's like asking which is my favourite kid. I can't do it.

TOMMY CULLINEN

I scored the UK version of their album *Aftermath* the weekend it came out, from an airline stewardess in April '66, and somehow ended up on the Stones' private jet with my friend Gayle Peterson, who knew the Standells and who said, 'Come out with me to the airport.'

In 1969 I hitchhiked over to Oakland Coliseum. A flatbed truck came, picked me up at the Burlingame Broadway exit and drove all the way over because they were heading over to the show. I laid down in the back of the truck, hallucinating without drugs during the bridge ride. I had enough money for an upper section ticket, costing $4.50, so I was in the house and Terry Reid was playing as I got there, which was pretty cool. He did a song called 'Friends' upon my entrance, and then BB King was awesome and beyond awesome were Ike and Tina Turner and the Ikettes.

So it was already a fantastic show and then on came the Rolling Stones, with Mick in his top hat. It was the best version of the band I ever saw, a raw and stripped down five-piece band with new guitar player Mick Taylor. The songs were already adrenaline-soaked and revolutionary in their lyrical content, and that Oakland Coliseum was the hottest place on earth.

Mick had the audience mesmerised. On the final encore he said, 'Come on San Francisco. Shake your asses. Let's see what you can do.' Everybody flew out of their seats and stood up for a rousing 'Street Fighting Man' and 'Satisfaction', and we got our satisfaction with a capital S.

It's in the top five shows of my life and I've seen over twelve hundred.

GREIL MARCUS, *ROLLING STONE*

We flooded into the Oakland Coliseum in 1969 with memories of the Cow Palace in 1966 – but this time there weren't any twelve-year-old kids kicking over the seats and wetting their pants. The sixties are over – the first thing that hit you when the Stones came out on stage was the evidence of the years in Mick Jagger's face. It seemed to have fallen into place for good. His features were no longer supple and loose; they were hard and thick, like the marble ridges of a statue. But that's a long way from the House of Wax. He still looked beautiful...

They ended it past three-thirty in the morning with 'Street Fighting Man.' Jagger seemed to draw himself up over his own height as he gestured for the words—the hall was fully lit, as if we were stealing a thrill from someone's closed-door idea of what the concert was supposed to be. It got away. Mick waved his arms until the crowd waved back and then stepped to the edge of the stage and blew astonishing kisses – with both hands – to everyone. Mick Jagger singing with his rock and roll band – a glorious moment.

I knew it had really happened that way when I got home around five A.M. Pinned to the icebox was a note: 'Just came by after the concert. *Wasn't it great!!!* We got within *five feet* of Mick!' And not without his help. In a way, that was the best part.

WAYNE ROBINS, *THE BERKELEY BARB*

Run down quick, stretch the legs. Stand around lobby, dig the crowd, the anticipation replaced by an anxious sense of now, of history. A fulfilment of dream, and you know it's going to happen any minute now. Any minute now, yet the tantalising moment of truth seems to be slipping away.

Promoter Bill Graham is centre stage, stalling. 'The Rolling Stones will be on next, so do what you gotta do, just remember, it's still illegal last I heard.' Graham's comment is regarded more joke than threat; they'd have to bust the whole building…

Graham is in master of ceremonies mode: 'I see Mr. Garcia in the audience,' giving a wave in the direction of where Jerry might be sitting. The audience applauds. 'I hate to sound like Ed Sullivan,' Graham says, 'but there's quite a few of the old guard here tonight.' I've written down the names of 'Quicksilver Messenger Service, the Dead, Joe Namath, Arturo Toscanini and Arthur Rimbaud.' I don't know if Graham actually said those names, or that under the influence of both Hunter Thompson (the writer) and Hunter Thompson (the prodigious drug user), whose hallucinatory level I tried to match that night, I just wrote those names down.

What Graham does say is, 'I know these things don't happen in the Bay Area, but please don't rush the stage, because you're excited, and that's cool, but you might be bumming out some other people, who won't say anything to you but will get you with their vibrations.'

One of the Stones' entourage comes out to announce, 'The boys arrived a trifle late,' and is answered by a surprising number of boos. This city has been excitedly cock-teased for the last week, amid some consternation about ticket prices, which went for $7.50 top, unless Graham did the same thing the promoter was said to have done in LA, which was to save the first 20 rows for trade, friends, press, favours, etc., an instant status symbol for those willing to pay $12.50 a shot. My ticket, in the last row of the highest section of Oakland Coliseum, was $6.

All week the Bay Area airwaves have been riddled with Rolling Stones music and almost nothing else; one station did a four-hour solid Stones' extravaganza, another interviewed Jagger in the studio. Ads every five minutes, though quite superfluous, because all tickets for both shows were sold out, and anybody who didn't know that the Rolling Stones would be at the Oakland Coliseum that week must have been so far away, so completely out of touch with our excuse for civilisation, that words would be wasted. Any minute now...

Any minute now, another apology, how the boys are getting themselves together, and will be out in 'literally two minutes'. The Stones' stage rep is good as his word. Two minutes, and 'Now, for rock 'n' roll,' the crowd erupts. It is Mick Jagger, alive and magical, in what I can only hope to describe as a red, white and blue outfit, like a peyote American flag, over a black jumpsuit, with a magnificent flowing fiery red scarf, long as a scarf anyway, but worn around the neck, like a necktie. On his head, an Uncle Sam hat, stripes from the night they drove old Dixie down. He waves it like a wand, bows like an electric enchanted swan, as if introducing himself: 'Pleased to meet you, hope you guessed my name.'

The closed-circuit TV screen, looming large above the stage, allows scrutiny of his facial movement: He moves like a ballet dancer who knows he's baaad. 'I was born in a crossfire hurricane,' he almost pouts; as 'Jumpin' Jack Flash' begins.

He's a bit off the beat, the Stones seeming to have trouble coordinating, hearing each other. Two amps are malfunctioning and microphones seem poorly placed. Mick apologises, but as far as The People are concerned, 'It's all right, in fact it's a gas.' Hip to the sound situation, Mick tells Keith to get his acoustic guitar while the amps are fixed. It's a duo, 'Prodigal Son', Mick and Keith on the Delta at *Beggar's Banquet.*

Almost apologetic for the low-key start of the set, Jagger assuredly tells the crowd to be patient, it will be worth it: 'When we get our electricity straight, we'll really get it on.' It sounded almost ominous. He meant it as the band launched into Chuck Berry's 'Oh Carol'. Keith Richards, headmaster of the Chuck Berry School of Guitar, picking quickly, carefully, waddling if not quite duck-walking. Charlie Watts drumming now into it, Bill Wyman, clean and coherent on bass, chewing gum as ever standing in some distant shadow. Mick Taylor, now synched with Keith's rhythm guitar, playing sure, creative tough leads. The mastery over 'Oh Carol' was total, and the audience responded with ecstatic applause. The crowd is stoned, of course, but stoned with respect, as if the band had been able you surpass the impossibly high expectations, a chord struck uniting audience and band beyond a musical or theatrical connection, a psychic platform on which the country's emergent stoned majority can climb on to. [Inscrutable handwriting here, something about John Lennon, Jesus, and a sold out resurrection at Disneyland, an event that had not actually occurred.]

Another acoustic blues followed, Robert Johnson's 'Love in Vain', from the new album, *Let It Bleed*. Jagger sounds almost solemn, declaring: 'It's something that we didn't write, but wish we did.'

The pace picks up with a show-stopping 'Sympathy for the Devil', if the show was stoppable; only another equipment glitch made it so. They toned it down for a harder edged, but still slow-paced 'I'm Free'. The new album, *Let It Bleed*, would not be released for nearly a month, but a new song played at Oakland will rank as one of Jagger-Richards all-time classics. It's called 'Midnight Rambler'. It starts with Mick blowing from the hips on harmonica, then singing with savage intent. Keith's playing ferocious rock blues, then things slow down while Mick raps out the lyrics, Charlie and Bill, who've slowed to inaudibility, pick the beat up again, and everyone in the arena's minds seem so blown you can almost see the brain matter on the Coliseum ceiling.

How do you top the debut of 'Midnight Rambler'? 'Honky Tonk Women' seems a good choice, especially as Jagger, at full throttle, suddenly shouts, 'Let me look at you! Let's see this audience!' The houselights go up and on the floor, a couple is dancing in the aisle, then two couples, then 30 couples, then the aisles are full of people dancing, and now it's really on: Back to the summer of 1965, rock and roll's best 3 minutes, 30 seconds, the audience exuberance belying the title: '(I Can't Get No) Satisfaction', and all is pandemonium. A cameraman with tripod is pulled on to the stage to save his equipment and his body from the surge, Jagger prancing back and forth, throwing kisses, waving his red scarf like a matador at the onrushing herd of bulls, people dancing on their chairs...

This is Oakland, birthplace of the Black Panther Party, and everyone knows that if they weren't being hosted by the government [in jail], Huey Newton, Eldridge Cleaver and Bobby Seale would be here in their hometown, digging the scene. Reading the vibe, the Stones see the electric multitude of 'power to the people' fists pumping the air, and the Stones pump back, with the only possible farewell: 'Street Fighting Man', any ambiguities of intent erased. And, before anyone can protest their departure, the house lights are on, muzak is on the loudspeakers, there's another show tomorrow night. What can a poor boy do that's just seen this rock and roll band? Go to the parking lot, ask for a ride back to San Francisco (done, and done), and get a little higher with the people.

TOM DONAHUE, *CASH BOX*

I've had a chance to see the Stones in their appearances in this country since I first presented them in concert in 1965 and it has been interesting to watch their evolvement. What started out as the Rolling Stones has become Mick Jagger and the Rolling Stones and with Brian's death Jagger's dominance has been emphasised to an even greater degree. Brian is sadly missed. On stage he was the other side of Jagger's coin. The softness for Mick's hard edge, the innocent reflection of Jagger's evil. Mick Taylor is probably a more accomplished musician and his influence is strongly felt in some of their new material, of which they performed quite a bit, with 'Midnight Rambler' sounding the best of all.

Jagger was on his whole Satanic trip, if you can imagine a bitchily dancing Lucifer who never stopped snapping his body or twirling his long red scarf which he alternately manipulated like a gay El Cordobes and a crazed Isadora Duncan. He climaxed the show by turning on the house lights so that the Stones could dig the crowd and the crowd could dig each other, then calling out to the 'Come on, San Francisco, let me see you shake your ass'. He brought them down the aisles for a frenzied finale of 'Little Queenie', 'Honky Tonk Women' and 'Street Fighting Man'.

The Stones make you happy all the way. Their rhythmic gut appeal has no competition. They remain the greatest rock and roll performing act in the world.

10 NOVEMBER 1969

SPORTS ARENA
SAN DIEGO
CALIFORNIA

"There have been a few punch ups in San Diego. But we managed to get the police outside of the concerts which makes it much cooler"

MICK JAGGER

"People didn't scream anymore. The music was taken seriously. In '69 you had proper amplification. Suddenly you could hear everybody. Nobody had heard drums before. We must have sounded a joke before. But in '69 you really had to be on top of it to play. That's how Hendrix and bands like Led Zeppelin came about. I call that tour 'the Led Zeppelin tour', because it was the first time we had to go on and play for an hour-and-a-half. I blame it on Jimmy Page. Led Zeppelin had come to the States, and they would do a twenty-minute drum solo and endless guitar solos"

CHARLIE WATTS

BRIAN NASH

My date and I were way back and up high in the San Diego Sports Arena for the first three acts (Terry Reid, Ike and Tina, BB King). Sadly, I don't remember much of any of their performances except Reid did 'Horses In A Rainstorm' and oddly, in my mind anyway, 'introduced' the band members before his last song as 'we're Terry Reid'.

As soon as the Stones started playing, we decided to move forward. We were back, on the ground floor along the right side of the arena, in a group of about 50 people, 100 feet from the stage and held back by security. After four songs the dam broke and we found ourselves about six feet from the stage, directly in front of Bill Wyman.

I wish I knew as much in what to look for in musicians back then as I do now. But I do remember Keith playing some fierce rhythm and Taylor slashing leads – although my best friend, who ended up a few feet away somehow – said that Keith played a lot of leads as well. At one point between songs, Mick pointed to Watts and remarked (mockingly? I'm not sure), 'Here's Charlie. He's our drummer.'

I recall Wyman being almost like a statue as Jagger danced around the stage, putting a bottom on the songs as someone who knew what he had to do and was going to do it without frills. Workmanlike. I also remember a small acoustic set in the middle; Jagger taking off his belt and smacking the floor in sync with the band during 'Midnight Rambler'; and Mick tossing small flowers at the audience at the show's end. I caught several small blossoms and kept them in a book for a few decades before I lost track.

The main thing that sticks in my mind is the energy. It was everywhere, on the stage and in the crowd. The music drove it, but the energy was like a thing in and of itself. It was something I'd never experienced before. The San Diego concert has been bootlegged many times, but the bootlegs fail to capture that 'energy' I describe above. The album *Get Yer Ya-Ya's Out!* also fails to do so, in my opinion. The closest is the bootleg album I have, *LiveR Than You'll Ever Be*, from a Bay Area concert two weeks before.

My friend and I often talk about the best concerts we saw back in the late sixties and early seventies. I don't count this among them. It wasn't so much a concert as an experience, like comparing coffee (regular concerts) to taking psychedelics.

PHILIP ELWOOD, *THE SAN FRANCISCO EXAMINER*

Mick Jagger and the Rolling Stones, thoroughly professional, rough and unsavory, wound up their audience to the breaking point at the Oakland Coliseum last night and then for the last twenty minutes of their hour and a quarter first-show appearance let everything and everybody unravel in an uproarious, aisle-filled, celebration of getting together.

The 20-year-old new Stone, guitarist Mick Taylor, plays strong single-line solos, almost as well as The Fish's Barry Melton, whom he somewhat resembles. On a 'Lonesome Station Blues' thing, Taylor almost outshone Jagger's vocal.

The crowd-exploders at the end of the Stones' set began with a dynamic 'Midnight Strangler', and 'Jumpin' Jack Flash', and then roared into 'Satisfaction', 'Honky Tonk Women', and the place erupted, into the aisles, down front... a minor amount of riotous rough stuff and a grand and glorious emotional explosion...

In contrast to the Saturday night Los Angeles presentation of the same show, which ended at 5 a.m. after frightful production hangups, poor amplification, and irresponsible conduct, last night's Bill Graham-produced event went off virtually without a hitch.

There was an over-stage closed circuit TV screen which gave everyone a close up of stage activity and, as usual, Graham didn't allow for foolishness in setting-up for the next act.

Although Jagger became quite exercised about some claimed electric failures on stage, the show's whole effect and pacing was one of the most pleasurable in recent memory for this observer.

11 NOVEMBER 1969

ARIZONA VETERANS MEMORIAL COLISEUM
PHOENIX
ARIZONA

"The crowd went ballistic when the lights went down"

STEVE FIEGEN

STEVE FIEGEN

The Rolling Stones were coming to the Coliseum. The buzz in high school was awesome. I had seen the Guess Who and Al Davis in concert there previously, and remembered that tickets were $5 each. But when I went to buy the tickets to the Stones, the price had doubled to $10 a ticket. Being a Stones fan since *The Ed Sullivan Show*, this meant little to me; I would have paid $20 each. Back then though, I was making $1.19 an hour. Though buying two tickets was tough, I did it regardless. Brian Jones and Keith Richards were my favourite guitarists. I played a Keith-style of guitar playing.

But the scuttlebutt in town wasn't as optimistic as I was. Between the conservative newscasts about drugs, booze, violence and the outrage over ticket costs, the Stones weren't getting much love from Phoenix. In fact, the show was not a sell-out. There were something like 4,000 seats vacant. People were picketing outside the Coliseum, with signs either blaming officials or the Stones themselves.

Our seats were pretty good, on the second row from the floor. We watched Terry Reid and then Ike and Tina Turner warm up as the opening acts. It was then an hour and a half wait after Tina's last song.

People were getting very restless, listening to old Stones albums, not to mention things were getting more physical outside the coliseum. About an hour and 45 minutes had gone by when they mentioned the Stones were in the building and the crowd lit up with a roar. There was a skinny long-haired person staring out from between the curtains and I remember people yelling, 'There's Mick!' It wasn't – it must have been a stage crew person. Then, all of a sudden, the lights all came on and from both entrances we saw hundreds of people filing into the place. I guess either the city promoters were afraid of the crowd busting down the doors, or they wanted the Stones to make sure they were playing to a full house. Either way, they let 4,000 people in for free.

The crowd went ballistic when the lights went down and you could see the silhouettes of the Stones getting on stage. Then the spotlight hit and there stood Mick Jagger, donning his American top hat and black Leo shirt. He apologised for the long wait and jumped into 'Jumpin' Jack Flash'. Mick Taylor looked like one of my high school friends, with his nervous boy-like grin. But his mastery on guitar was amazing. He played that SG on most of the show. He did something in that hour and half show that few had ever done. He became my favourite guitarist of all time.

Jagger held everyone's attention with his charismatic dancing and singing. They went into 'Honky Tonk Women' and I swear I thought the bleachers were going to cave in. 'Love in Vain' was very close to the recorded version. 'Midnight Rambler' was the show-stopper, with Jagger using his scarf as a whip during the slow bluesy part. Again, they let Mick Taylor show off his blues prowess and the slow part seemed like about two minutes long. After 'Midnight Rambler', they jumped into 'Sympathy for the Devil'. Again, the bleachers rocked. When I listen to *Get Yer Ya-Ya's Out*, that's what it sounded like in Phoenix. Nobody sat down the rest of the concert, all the way through to the final number, 'Street Fighting Man'. Jagger threw flowers at the audience and on the band members, and the crowd went wild as the Stones left the stage. Everyone lit cigarette lighters to try and get the Stones to do another song, but there was no encore.

My friend who came with me, who was never a big Stones fan, told me it was the best concert he had ever seen. The Stones were on that night and they rocked sleepy town Phoenix, Arizona.

JOAN MCNAMARA

I was there. They didn't sell out.

REID ELLIOTT

Terry Reid was the opener, followed by the Ike and Tina Revue. I had just turned 15, so my memory has abandoned me with this show. I had been going to concerts since 1968: Blue Cheer opening for Eric Burdon and The Animals was my first concert, followed by the Mothers of Invention opening for the Chambers Bros, then The Doors, Iron Butterfly, Blind Faith… The list goes on. The Rolling Stones is one of the least memorable of all the shows I had been to. I think I was more taken with Ike and Tina. I do recall thinking that the Rolling Stones audio sound system was bad compared to previous shows I had attended at the Coliseum.

KAREN SCHMITZ MAGGIO

There were people sneaking into seats down low and fights kept breaking out when they wouldn't move. One pair of guys went over the railing - and that was before the show! Ike and Tina tore the place up.

The Stones were so late. When they finally came on, it was pitch black and a little pink point lit the stage. It grew until a caped figure could be seen. Mick threw back the cape and popped on a top hat. I won't ever forget that.

13 NOVEMBER 1969

MOODY COLISEUM
UNIVERSITY PARK
DALLAS
TEXAS

"It was a very stripped down, lean sound and the lighting was two or three follow spots and one or two floodlights"

MIKE HASKINS

MIKE HASKINS

This was the first Rolling Stones concert in Dallas. They had played Fort Worth back in 1965, but I was only eleven years old then, and I was yet to become a Stones fan, so I didn't attend. (I bought my first Stones album, *December's Children*, in December '65). When I heard that the Stones would be playing in Dallas in November '69, I was excited. I was also a fan of Terry Reid, and he was the opening act! I was only familiar with second-billed Chuck Berry as a songwriter, and wasn't convinced of his high-energy showmanship until I saw him in person.

I didn't know what to expect from the 1969 version of the Stones. I had heard earlier that summer that Brian Jones left the Stones in June, then died almost immediately in July. This was mind-boggling. The idea of the Stones without Jones was unimaginable. Wasn't he one of the main guys? The Stones had no recent LP release to check out. *Beggar's Banquet* had been released December '68, a year before. Honky Tonk Women was a #1 hit single in the summer of '69, but there was no new LP to back it up. What would they sound like live? What songs would they play? I was familiar with the new guy, Mick Taylor, from his albums with John Mayall in 1967-68. He was a brilliant blues guitarist, but how would he fit into the Stones?

The show was booked into Moody Coliseum at SMU (Southern Methodist University) in Dallas. I had seen the Jefferson Airplane there in the summer of '68, and Moody was a basketball arena, with all the poor-quality acoustics that you might expect.

Since I was only 15 years old, and too young to drive, I convinced my mom to drive me 30 minutes in to Dallas to buy tickets from the ticket window outside a large bank building (these were different times). Balcony level seats were $3 to $4; not cheap by 1969 standards.

Terry Reid played a solid, brief, five-song set. Chuck Berry played a longer, hard rocking set, debuting his soon-to-be smash hit, the embarrassingly abominable 'My Ding-A-Ling'. (It went on to become his only #1 hit record! Who would have believed it?).

Then, we waited... a long time… at least an hour, maybe 90 minutes. Frisbees were thrown around the audience. I thought, 'They should bring Terry Reid back on to play another set. Why not?' Finally, the Stones came on and opened with a gut-punch loud 'Jumpin' Jack Flash'. I guess that answered how they would sound.

The Stones were sporting a backline of brand-new prototype Ampeg SVT 300-watt amps. They had five large speaker cabinets per man. They were loud! Even with the crappy arena acoustics, I could hear the lyrics and every instrument pretty clearly.

The set list was standard 1969 selections. Notably though, they didn't play 'I'm Free'. When I later heard that they often included 'I'm Free' in their set on that tour, I couldn't imagine why they would have bothered… I'm still wondering.

The Stones performed several unfamiliar, previously unreleased, songs. 'Love in Vain', 'You Gotta Move', 'Midnight Rambler' and 'Live With Me' were all instantly memorable on first hearing. The *Let It Bleed* LP wasn't released until two weeks after the show.

The band only included the five Stones, plus Ian Stewart on piano for 'Little Queenie' and 'Honky Tonk Women'. There were no horns, no backup singers, no extra keyboards. It was a very stripped down, lean sound and the lighting was two or three follow spots and one or two floodlights. Very basic, nothing automated.

The set was pretty short by contemporary standards, 60 - 70 minutes. However, the Stones' previous 1964 - 66 shows were usually much shorter, more like 30 minutes.

A good time was had!

SET LIST

Jumpin' Jack Flash
Carol
Sympathy for the Devil
Stray Cat Blues
Love in Vain
Prodigal Son
You Gotta Move
Under My Thumb
Midnight Rambler
Live with Me
Little Queenie
(I Can't Get No) Satisfaction
Honky Tonk Women
Street Fighting Man

THOMAS NOBLE

They did their hits at the time and I seem to remember Jagger taking off his jacket and tossing it into the audience. But that was a long time ago and these years just flow by like a broken-down dam!

CHRIS RHODES

Chuck Berry played with them. I remember him duck walking across the stage while he played. The Stones debuted some *Let it Bleed* songs – 'Midnight Rambler', 'Love In Vain' – and 'Sympathy For The Devil', 'Satisfaction' and 'Honky Tonk Women'. I'm foggy about what else they played. My ticket cost me ten dollars.

GARY TACKEL

It was a smaller venue, and a great place to see the Stones. Chuck Berry opened. The Stones were at their best with Mick Taylor on lead – all the members of the band were at the top of their game. Mick was in his black 'devil' outfit, with a red sash around his waist. They turned the house lights on for the last songs, and it didn't dampen the crowd's spirits one bit!

JAMES M SMITH

What Gary doesn't mention is that we got to Moody to find he had left the tickets at home. Luckily, we were early and he was able to make the trip home to fetch them and get back in time.

JANELL OLIVER MYERS

That was probably the closest I've ever been to the stage and I have seen them many times. It's my favourite Stones era; their clothes, the music, the crowds that were matching the vibes. Terry Reid was young and his music is still something I remember. Chuck was a bit raunchy for the times, which was surprising. The Stones were phenomenal and dare I say, seemed 'altered', but it was 1969…

CINDY MCGREGOR GREEN

So many people stood on their chairs that it was hard to see. That's the only time I remember that happening in all of my concert attending years. I guess no one could contain their excitement.

KAROLINA MAYO

Terry Reid did 'Superlungs My Supergirl', Chuck Berry ducked walked, and the Stones came on extremely late. I missed most, if not all, of the show waiting in line for the pay phone, waiting to call my parents to tell them I would be late getting home. I was 15 and my parents expected me home by midnight. 1969, the age before cell phones.

KENT HOFMEISTER

I was a freshman at SMU and ushered the concert in exchange for a free pass.

14 NOVEMBER 1969

MEMORIAL COLISEUM
AUBURN
ALABAMA

"I don't think the jocks with their dates were ready for Mick Jagger"

RICK FREEMAN

RICK FREEMAN

I was two weeks shy of my sixteenth birthday. I paid $5.50 for my ticket. I remember the long wait to see them and how cold it was. The 6.30pm show didn't start until around 9pm, and the second show started after 11pm. As we entered the building, they announced that they had extended the curfew for students, which received a huge ovation from the students. I was dressed in jeans, a t-shirt and a denim jacket, while the students were wearing ties. Due to the late start, Terry Reid was cancelled. Chuck Berry opened the show and he was pure rock 'n' roll. He played like no one ever, pure rock at its finest.

The Stones finally came out, opening with 'Jumpin' Jack Flash'. I don't think the jocks with their dates were ready for Mick Jagger. I certainly was not! What an entertainer. But what was more interesting to me was Keith Richards. He had so much charisma you could not take your eyes off him. His playing was sublime. The rest of the band held down the fort while Mick and Keith took centre stage. That said, Mick Taylor proved what a wonderful player he is. 'Love in Vain' is the song I remember because of his slide playing and Jagger's singing. In fact, the three blues they did are the ones I remember best. First was 'Prodigal Son' followed by 'You Gotta Move', both played with Mick and Keith sitting on stools and Charlie adding percussion, and then 'Love in Vain'.

'Midnight Rambler' was a breath taker that had people spellbound. Girls who looked like they should be in church were screaming while their dates seemed confused, especially when Jagger took off his belt and hit the floor with it. 'Satisfaction' was another favourite.

The show ended and they didn't play an encore. People do not realise that most acts didn't always play an encore back then. Now they are planned in advance.

Music journalist Michael Lydon wrote that the southern dates were the low point of the 1969 tour. This was during the era when most thought the south was as it's portrayed in the movie *Easy Rider*. But the Stones recorded three of their all-time greatest songs – 'Brown Sugar', 'Wild Horses' and 'You Gotta Move' – whilst in Alabama at the mecca of soul music, Muscle Shoals.

I remember that the Stones having trouble with airline reservations and their flight had flown away empty from Dallas to Auburn on instructions from an unknown source. Things were not as organised as they are today.

15 NOVEMBER 1969

ASSEMBLY HALL
UNIVERSITY OF ILLINOIS
CHAMPAIGN
ILLINOIS

"I was too cheap to take a girl that I didn't even know to see the Stones"

MIKE HANSEN

NANCY FLOM

As a teenager in the sixties, the Rolling Stones were hard to miss. There was the whole 'clean cut' Beatles versus the 'bad boys' Stones thing. I loved the music, everything from the top 40 they played on WLS out of Chicago to the more album-oriented groups like the Stones or The Who. Of course, 'Sugar Sugar' was #1 in the fall of 1969. Ugh! I loved everything but that.

I was a senior at the University of Illinois that fall. My friend, Karen, and I had tickets to attend the big anti-war moratorium march in Washington, DC, but at nearly the last minute, she chickened out. Those tickets were $25 a piece, a lot of money for a college student back then, and weren't refundable (I was making $2.25 an hour plus tips, working in a campus club serving college students $1.25 pitchers of beer and sloe gin fizzes). I remember thinking, 'Oh, well, might as well go see the Stones,' who were scheduled to play at the Assembly Hall the same day as the moratorium, November 15th.

Two friends agreed to go with me, and I was able to score tickets to the afternoon show. If memory serves (and it may not), they were $16.50 a piece, still a princely sum back then. Even though it was pretty last minute, I don't recall having any problems getting them, although they were in C section, the worst in the house (the Assembly Hall is shaped like a disc).

The show started two and a half hours late. Rumours were swirling around that their equipment was late in arriving, but I don't recall any official announcement. My friend, Maggie, got up to go to the bathroom and was gone for a very long time. She was so high (probably acid – the pot back then wasn't much, at least not in Champaign-Urbana) that she got lost trying to find her way back to our seats. Everyone was pretty fed up by the time the show finally started. I can imagine that the people who had tickets for the second show probably weren't too happy about standing around out in the cold, waiting to be let in either (no texts in those days – only word of mouth to let people know about the delay).

BB King and Terry Reid were the opening acts, and then the Stones took the stage. I remember Mick wearing a shirt with the Greek letter Omega on it. The concert was fantastic. I wish I had appreciated at the time how lucky I was to see Mick and the boys in their prime, but what young person thinks to take the time to appreciate such things? I do recall the crowd as being pretty sedate. Most people stayed in their seats, which was typical for the Assembly Hall. I think the crowd for the second show was much more lively, and congregated in front of the stage.

If I close my eyes, I can still see Mick stalking the stage during 'Midnight Rambler', one of my favourite songs.

I saw the Stones again in San Francisco on their *Voodoo Lounge* tour. It was quite a different experience, with the outdoor venue and the big screen, so people in the back could actually see the band.

Both of the friends I went to the concert with are long dead, one from alcoholism and suicide, the other from cancer. A lot has changed since college, but I still love the music. Today's music ain't got the same soul, you know?

MIKE HANSEN

They were supposed to perform two shows that evening. One I think was at 5pm, and the other one at 8pm. The first show was over two hours late in starting. Everyone was mad. When they finally started, no one would stand or cheer for them, until Mick Jagger yelled, 'I want to see you people move your asses.' The place erupted. They wouldn't let anyone in for the second show until the first one was over. They waited over two hours outside to get in.

I was supposed to have a blind date that night and to pick her up at 8pm. I called her from a pay phone and said I had car trouble. I know she heard Mick Jagger singing in the background. I was too cheap to take a girl that I didn't even know to see the Stones.

RICHARD DERK

I photographed the first show for the *Daily Illini*. The crowd was quite polite, at the urging of the Assembly Hall management. I was at the front of a rather low, simple stage. After three or four songs, Mick Jagger stepped to the mic and yelled, 'Hey, Champaign-Urbana, get up off your asses,' and the band launched into a thrilling performance of 'Midnight Rambler'.

The crowd surged forward, a large mass of humanity, and it was obvious I was in trouble as in I might be crushed into the stage. A large Stones bodyguard reached down and grabbed me under my arms and pulled me up on the stage. He put me to the side behind an amp and said, 'Stay here, don't move.' I stayed there and got some very nice images from the stage with Mick and the crowd beyond him. One ran in *Rolling Stone*, which at that time was quite a thrill for me. Since then, I have photographed or attended nine other Stones shows, but that first one was one of the real wild experiences of my photojournalism career.

MIKE BLEICH

It was my first rock concert experience. We made the trip to Champaign from Macomb, where I was a freshman at Western Illinois University. We arrived a bit late at the concert, just as many of the fans from the upper sections began to rush the floor. We stood and watched the remainder of the opening act, BB King, and the entire Stones concert from somewhere on the floor. I remember Mick dancing around the stage in his black cape.

KEN BUS

Mick Jagger looked up at the shape of Assembly Hall and said, 'I feel like I've been swallowed by a giant clam.'

VEDA BARRETT

Mick Jagger threw long red roses to the crowd. Someone threw them back on stage and Mick walked off. He was done!

STAN JAMES

I was a junior in high school when four friends and I went to the Rolling Stones concert. It was the first time I had gone to an event at the Assembly Hall. I recall we had seats in C section and the place was full of people. During the concert it was hard to hear most of the song lyrics due to all the noise coming from the crowd. I remember huge rolled joints being passed around (I didn't partake) and wondered why no one was telling people to stop doing so.

Keith Richards seemed to be feeling ill or was on something, as he stayed in the background much of the show.

My sense of the concert when it ended was that they really didn't sound much like their recordings and, other than Mick prancing about during their show, I was not too impressed. After the concert, one of our group had heard the Stones were staying in Urbana at a hotel, and we all should go find them. We didn't go looking for them; instead, we headed back to Rantoul.

I still listen to their music and find it amazing they are still well known and playing to huge crowds.

P LARRY NELSON

I started out sitting in a section above the main floor, and then at some point, after a break maybe, I and others started moving down onto the floor in front of the stage. Pot smoke was everywhere. No need to light up when all you needed to do was inhale the air around you.

DEBBIE STEWART

What a killer show! I was 16. The day of the show, I was running a 103 temperature and had bronchial pneumonia but crawled out of the house to see one of the best shows EVER! It was magic!

PATTY HENDRIX CHICOINE

I was not a Stones fan, but my boyfriend was, so we went. There were two concerts scheduled, back-to-back. Fortunately, we had tickets to the earlier concert. For reasons that I do not think were ever explained to the crowd, the Stones did not take the stage until nearly two hours after their scheduled time. The Stones being the Stones, I think we all thought it was drug- or alcohol-related, but the truth was probably more mundane.

When the Stones finally took the stage, the angry crowd quieted to a dull roar and got into the spirit of the famous rock band. Our seats were very high up, but there was no question which performer was Jagger when he came out on stage. The man gyrated mercilessly and reminded me of what a chicken with its head cut off might look like. The concert did nothing to turn me into a Stones fan, but those who came in loving the group probably still loved them when the concert ended.

It was quite cold, and those who were to attend the second concert had to wait outside in that cold until the first concert cleared out. I assume most arrived well in advance of the scheduled second concert time, so they had to wait an additional approximate two hours in very cold weather. As we left the first concert, we had to push through the huddled angry masses who were waiting for the second concert. And, in good faith, I could not even tell them it was worth waiting for.

CRAIG PETTY

I was a huge fan, mainly of Brian Jones, and I was unsure if the Stones were going to still be cool. My friend borrowed his mom's car in the late morning to 'go buy a pair of shoes' and we drove out of town 200 miles to see the Stones!

They were playing two shows and the first show was supposed to be an afternoon show that didn't start until late afternoon, like 5pm or 6pm. We got floor seats on the day for $7.50. That was about two bucks more than any show to that date. My friends went home after the first show but I stayed without a ride home, walked around the crowd and found another friend who was going to the second show (so I went home with them).

I tried to sneak my camera in but got busted. They had me wait in a room with a bunch of others who also had cameras. But when they turned their backs, I bolted out the door and into the dark arena.

For the first show I was surprised how animated Mick was. The crowd surged the stage at the beginning of 'Midnight Rambler', which was new and previously unheard. I landed with my elbows on the stage right in front of Keith. He only came up to his mic during 'Honky Tonk Women' and I reached up and touched his snakeskin-booted foot. He looked down at me and laughed!

During the second show the crowd rushed immediately forward and I was in front of Mick Taylor this time. It was so loud I thought my head was going to cave in.

KATY MCLEOD

I saw them play in four cities on the '69 tour. I've got a tour button that would get you backstage, get you helicopter passes. It was worth its weight in gold. The sound technician was on the floor working the boards and for some reason he liked my friend's belt and he said, 'What can I give you for that belt?' And my friend said, 'Your button.'

My friend immediately went backstage wearing that button in Champaign, Illinois. 20 of us had driven the 200 miles from St Louis up to Champaign, Illinois. My brother was there. My best friend was there. All my best friends were there. It's the best show I've ever seen in my entire life. We were all crushed up in front. There's a picture taken by Ethan Russell, which he used for the cover of his book about the 1969 tour, and you can see us all in the picture. It was like we were on stage with them. My elbows were on the stage. The experience was just phenomenal.

16 NOVEMBER 1969

INTERNATIONAL AMPHITHEATRE
CHICAGO
ILLINOIS

"In Chicago, it was just like last time (1966): a lot of screamers, a lot of young girls, really young, like 12 or 14. And other places there were some who don't listen to the music at all; it's just a fantasy experience for them. Like in Boston, that crowd had almost an identical response to what they gave us last time. But on the coast, and a lot of other places, there was a very large cross section of people, all kinds of people, and they *listened.* A lot of them did. That was new in some ways"

MICK JAGGER

KATY MCLEOD

From Champaign, Illinois I took a train 100 miles to Chicago and checked into their hotel. We stayed at the Ambassador in Chicago. Wherever the Stones stayed, we stayed. We made a career out of following the Stones. We wouldn't bother them. We went down to the restaurant. We got seated in a booth right near theirs.

The show was fabulous but there was a stream of ushers between us and the stage. I don't think we sat down on our seats ever. We were very close to the stage. I took a picture of Mick in his top hat when he first came on stage.

MARY GLUSAK

It was at the International Amphitheater, a dumpy arena on the grounds of the old Chicago Stock Yards. No more afternoon shows: they had enough of a catalogue to play a whole concert. I tried to write down some songs but writing was getting in the way of seeing the show from backstage. I was an usherette, but wasn't able to get close to anyone, but I really didn't want to with all the pandemonium: there was lots of liquor and weed. (Gasp!) I was able to sneak a couple of friends into the venue after the opening act (I can't remember who opened) and these goofs tried to jump the stage, but were carried off by big guy ushers. I never got them in for free again.

KAREN L RYBAK

My whole life all I ever heard was, 'How could you like Mick Jagger? He's so ugly.' My mom called him 'skinny ass'!

In 1965 my cousin Bob who lived in California visited me in Chicago and brought the album *Aftermath* for me to listen to and that was the beginning of my love for the Stones. My favourite song on the album was 'Under My Thumb', and it's still my favourite song. I played it over and over.

In September of 1969 I got married. I was 21. My husband was (as I called it) a fruit gum music fan. We definitely did not agree on music. I listened to Jimi Hendrix, Deep Purple and of course The Beatles. But my heart was with the Stones. The bad boys, as they were called.

I loved everything about them. I followed all the news about them and bought every magazine they were in. I had every single and every album. (I now have a Stones-themed music room and all my walls are covered with pictures and paintings and my framed album covers.)

My husband worked at a mall where they had a Ticketron. I had heard the Stones were coming to Chicago so had him get tickets for us and our two friends. We wore our new hip hugger pants which were the craze then. We were so cool!

Our seats were on the floor, about halfway back. I can't remember for sure but I believe Chuck Berry was the opening act. They also had Ike and Tina Turner as an opening act. The concert was awesome. Mick did the cherry picker above the audience and threw rose petals down from a bucket. I have some saved in my jewellery box. At the end of the show, we rushed the stage for 'Satisfaction' so I was very near.

When they next came to Chicago, I had just had my first baby so didn't go. It's the only tour I missed. For the 1981 tour, I won tickets from a radio station. I was the tenth caller and correctly answered who sang with Carly Simon on 'You're So Vain'. It was Mick Jagger!

BENJAMIN KREPACK

With two of my best friends, we had to be the three youngest fans in this colossal cauldron of a building just adjacent to the Chicago stock yards on the city's south side, not too far from where we all lived. This enormous arena, with the slight stench of elephant shit still lingering in the air from the Barnum and Bailey Circus that the place was better known for, was now filled up with thousands of teenagers ready to rock.

I'd be turning 14 in five days, but this day was like a hundred birthdays rolled into one. THIS WAS MY VERY FIRST ROCK CONCERT! I remember having to beg and cajole my parents to go. And astonishingly, they finally and reluctantly relented, despite a deep concern about letting their son loose onto their dreaded perceived hippy orgy of a rock concert.

As a music fan since I was eight, the Stones were secretly my favourite rock band. Everyone thought it was The Beatles who, of course, I still loved and adored. The Fabs started everything. Like a first love. But the Stones were a different universe altogether, intriguing and untouchable. My problem was simply that nobody would ever buy me a Stones album. For all my birthdays and holiday gifts, it was always Beatles, Beatles, Beatles. I even got a Dave Clark 5 single once! But never a Stones record for me. I had to finally take things into my own hands and at the age of ten I had finally saved enough dough from my weekly allowance to buy the album *Aftermath*. Now I couldn't wait for the day to see them in concert.

That day had finally come.

As I later learned, it was the great blues guitarist BB King and Ike and Tina Turner that were opening a lot of the shows on this tour. I was oblivious to all of it. In fact, it never occurred to me that there would even be an opening act. Suddenly the lights went out, people started shouting and whooping it up, and an announcer introduced 'Chuck Berry!' to the stage! It was almost too good to be true.

Chuck did a pretty short set and my buddies and me of course knew most of the songs he was playing. We certainly knew what a huge influence he had on the earlier Stones records prior to them starting to write their own material. Seeing Chuck come out before the band that helped boost his profile for younger music fans felt like perfect symmetry.

Soon enough, the Stones were announced, and they came out like a blaze of light, unzipping the dark. 'Jumpin' Jack Flash' sounded like I had never heard it before.

The concert was everything I thought it would be. In fact, it was a gas. They blasted through their set, one fantastic song after another.

In the middle of the show, we saw the curtains close and, with just Keith on a stool and with Mick standing at his side, they sang a couple of acoustic blues numbers, 'Prodigal Son' and 'You Gotta Move'. The curtains reopened and there were Charlie, Bill and Mick Taylor right where we last left them. They kicked in with 'Under My Thumb', followed by a long and dramatic 'Midnight Rambler'.

As I walked into the arena, a concert poster was shoved into my arms. No money exchanged, no merchandise table, just a guy handing out the posters for free. It was the official tour poster of the '69 tour, a drawing of an almost naked woman. Somehow, someway, I managed to hang on to that very poster and it currently is framed in the living room where my wife and I live.

I've seen the Stones a couple dozen more times over the next six decades. I've seen better shows, I often had better seats. The sound system was usually improved. But I still have a special place in my heart for that very first special show.

RAYMOND A VANLANOT

I took two other friends and we sat in our nosebleed seats. Terry Reid opened for them, and I turned into a Terry Reid fan immediately. But when the Stones hit the stage, they started up with 'Sympathy For The Devil' and Mick was looking up at me, and I was looking down at him with binoculars.

It was an amazing night. The Stones were loud, Keith was playing in his own way and running after Mick the whole concert. They were definitely the show makers. It was great to see Charlie Watts and Bill Wyman. I am not sure who was there as back up guitar, but it was not Ronnie Wood!

But, basically, I saw *the* band. I will never forget it.

TONY ROZENSKY

Chicago International Amphitheatre was right next to the slaughterhouse and was used for rodeos and conventions. Needless to say, the sound was shit for concerts but I remember being excited to see them.

The warm up acts were Terry Reid and Chuck Berry. Chuck was the perennial showman and Terry was promoting *Bang Bang You're Terry Reid*. I was less than 75 feet from the stage. I'm not gay, but I can say that Mick Taylor was the prettiest one on the stage. The Stones played a lot of songs from *Let It Bleed* which hadn't been released so there was some confusion, at least on my part. (I still think 'Midnight Rambler' sucks, but I have gone on to appreciate the rest of the LP.) The most interesting anecdotes I've heard were from the girls in my seventh or eighth grade classes who paid five or ten dollars and got to go backstage and meet a lot of British Invasion groups, including the Stones, and came back with pictures. A guy I once worked with claims he gave Mick Jagger bus or train fare years ago and that Mick never paid him back.

MARK THOMPSON

My memories are clear as an azure sky of deepest summer. My friend Harry and I showed up with no tickets and I said, 'Give me the best seats you got!'. The guy laughed at us, sold us VIP seats third row centre and said, 'Okay, enjoy the show!'

Terry Reid and Chuck Berry opened. Nobody knew or cared about Reid. After Chuck, who was fabulous, we had a nice two hour wait before the stones came on. It seemed like two hours, anyway. The guy sitting next to my pal Harry was a photographer. He gave me his card in case I wanted some pics, but young and dumb carried the day.

Keith Richards played his clear guitar for most of the show. I don't remember seeing or hearing a piano (although Ian Stewart was apparently playing on some numbers). I saw the Stones four times after that, but nothing could top this. And all for $7.25 per ticket.

MICK JAGGER

Chicago was incredible. The people there have so much energy, they are into doing so many things. You sometimes think it is all happening in England, then you realise it's mostly happening in the States.

THE ROLLING STONES 1969 TOUR

18 NOVEMBER 1969

THE ED SULLIVAN SHOW
CBS TELEVISION CITY STUDIOS
LOS ANGELES
CALIFORNIA

"These boys are hot, especially with the younger crowd. They're on a concert tour, so I decided to come here and tape them. They cost a lot of money, but they're worth it"

ED SULLIVAN

THE ROLLING STONES
in concert
BYRD
Nov. 7
Col. State Univ.
Ft. Collins, Colorado
Nov. 8
Forum
Los Angeles, California
Nov. 9
Oakland Coliseum
Oakland, California
Nov. 10
Sports Arena
San Diego, California
Nov. 11
Coliseum
Phoenix, Arizona
Nov. 13
Moody Coliseum
Dallas, Texas
Nov. 14
Coliseum
Auburn, Alabama
Nov. 15
U. of Illinois
Champaign, Ill.
Nov. 16
Chicago International
Amphi-Theater, Ill.
Nov. 20
Forum
Los Angeles, California
Nov. 24
Olympia Stadium
Detroit, Michigan
Nov. 25
Spectrum
Philadelphia, Pennsylvania
Nov. 26
Baltimore Civic Center
Baltimore, Maryland
Nov. 27 (Eve), 28 (Mat. & Eve)
Madison Sq. Garden
New York, New York
Nov. 29
Boston Gardens
Boston, Mass.
Nov. 30
Palm Beach International Raceway
Palm Beach, Florida

ROLLING STONES

NOVEMBER 6, 1969	EHB MONCK	LEAVE: LOS ANGELES
THURSDAY	PRODUCTION CREW	TIME: 8:10 AM
FORT. COLLINS, COL	BELMONT	FLITE; CONT AIR # 18
	IAN STEWART	ARR: DENVER
		TIME: 11:05 AM
	TRANSPORTATION	TO: COL. STATE UNIV.
	3 WAGS/1-20 FT VAN	ARR; 12:30 N
	EQUIPMENT/AIR	ARR: 11/5
	2 DIMMER BDS	
	8 SUPER TROUPS	
(209) 466-3993	HOTEL-	
	HOLIDAY INN	
	I-25 & HWY 14	
	FT. COLLINS	
LOCAL CONTACT	HOUSE CALL	TIME: 12:30
BARRY FEY	COL STATE UNIV	
(303) 744-6996	GYM	
	(303) 491-5276	
NOVEMBER 7	BAND	LEAVE: LOS ANGELES
FRIDAY	ENTOURAGE	TIME: 11:20 AM
		FLITE: CONT AIR # 26
		ARR: DENVER
		TIME: 2:15 PM
	TRANSPORTATION	LEAVE: DENVER-DRIVE 60 MI.
	4 LIMOS/1 WAGON	ARR; FT. COLLINS
		TIME: APPROX. 3:30PM
	REHEARSAL	TIME: APPROX 4:00PM
	CSU GYM	
	FULL SOUND	
	AMPLIFICATION	
	STAGE DRESSINGS	
	LIGHTS	

Beatles

The Beatles? "I think it's possible for them to do a to Mick has said it before, but worth repeating . . . the Beat are primarily a recording gro

"Even though they drew biggest crowds of their era in No America, I think the Beatles h passed their performing peak ev before they were famous. They a recording band, while our sce is the concerts and many of records were roughly made, on p pose. Our sort of scene is to ha a really good time with the au ence.

"It's always been the Ston thing to get up on stage and k the crap out of everything. We h three years of that before we ma it, and we were only just getti it together when we became famo We still had plenty to do on sta and I think we still have. Tha why the tour should be such groove for us."

(previous page) 1969 tour poster; (these pages, clockwise from top left) 1969 tour itinerary; Keith tells it to the *NME; Live'r Than You'll Ever Be* was a bootleg of the Oakland show; List of promoters for the first part of the tour; Mike Arenas was at Inglewood Forum

ROLLING STONE'S TOUR

November 7th - Colorado State University, Ft. Collins, Colorado - 10,300 seats - Gross potential, $60,000 - $35,000 against 65% - Promoter, Barry Fey.

November 8th - Forum, Los Angeles, California - 16,000 seats - Gross potential, $135,000 each show - $75,000 against 65% - Promoter, Concert Associates.

November 9th - Oakland Coliseum, Oakland, California - 20,000 seats Gross potential, $80,000 - $40,000 against 65% - Promoter, Bill Graham

November 10th - Sports Arena, San Deigo, California - 12,000 seats - Gross potential, $80,000 - $35,000 against 65% - Promoter, Bill Graham

November 13th - Moody Coliseum, Dallas, Texas - 8500 seats - Gross potential, $60,000 - $35,000 against 65% - Promoter, Concerts West.

November 14th - Coliseum, Auburn University, Auburn, Alabama - 10,000 seats - Gross potential, $80,000 - $35,000 against 70% - Promoter, Auburn University

November 15th - to be advised. Univ. of Illinois

November 16th - Chicago International Amphi-Theatre, Chicago, Illinois - 13,000 per show - Gross potential, $120,000 to $140,000 - $60,000 against 65% - Promoter, Frank Freid.

November 24th - Olympia Stadium, Detroit, Michigan - 17,000 seats - Gross potential, $90,000 to $100,000 - $50,000 against 65% - Promoter, Linke Cavalieri.

November 25th - Spectrum, Philadelphia, Pa. - 17,000 seats - Gross potential, $110,000 - $50,000 against 65% - Promoter, Herb Spivak and Moe Septee

November 26th - Baltimore Civic Center, Baltimore, Maryland - 12,189 seats - Gross potential, $70,000 - $35,000 against 65% - Promoter, Dave Cohan.

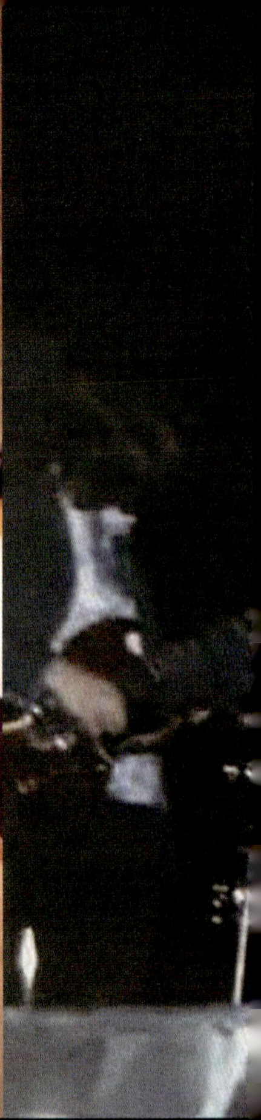

GRAND FUNK

Railroad

SMU McFARLIN AUDITORIUM

SATURDAY, NOV. 1, 8 P.M.

Tickets $3 and $4. Limited number available at Preston Ticket Agency, Coghill Simmons (both locations), Preston Record Center, Minsky's Music and Exchange Park Ticket Agency. Mail orders accepted.

First Choice Seats for the Rolling Stones Concert to Grand Funk Ticket Holders

ROLLING·STONES

THEIR ONLY APPEARANCE IN THE 10 STATE SOUTHWEST AREA!

NOV. 13, 8 P.M.

SMU MOODY COLISEUM

Tickets $7.50, $6.50, $5.50 and $4.00. Mail orders only to Preston Ticket Agency, P. O. Box 12000, Dallas 75225. Include stamped, self-addressed envelope with cashier's check or money order.

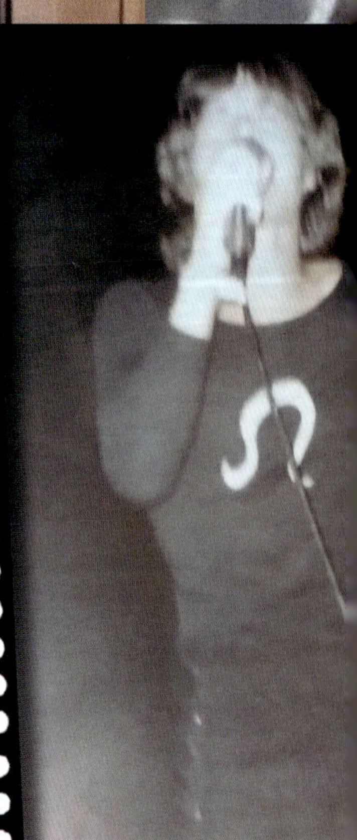

(clockwise from top left) Steve Fiegen saw the Stones rock sleepy Phoenix; the Stones in Dallas (Elaine Bender); Mike Haskins was at SMU & had to wait 90 minutes for the Stones to appear; Mick in Dallas (Elaine Bender); Ad for the SMU Moody Coliseum show

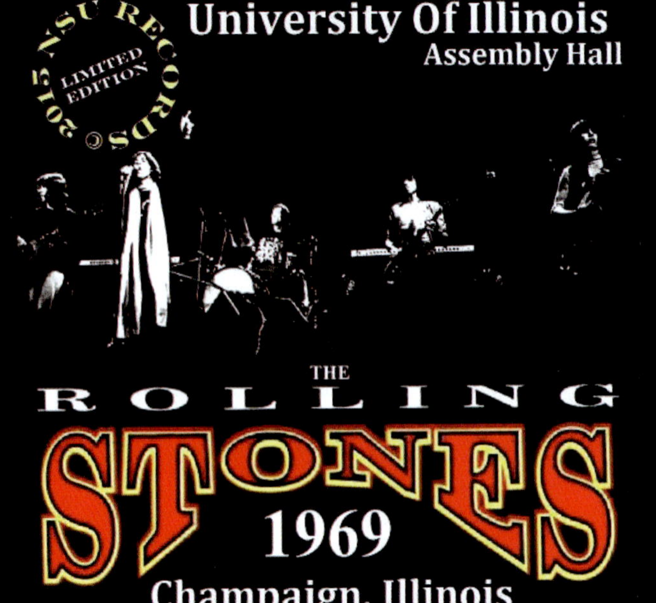

(clockwise from top left) Champaign bootleg; *Gimme Shelter poster*; The Daily Illini's coverage of the Champaign, Illinois gig; Students queue for Stones tickets at Champaign, Illinois (University of Illinois); Katy MacLeod's friend scored a tour button which gave backstage access; (next page) Mick in action at West Palm Beach (Ken Davidoff)

The
olling
tones

Keith Richard

Mick Taylor

Charlie Watts

Bill Wyman

Mick Jagger

The Rolling Stones (got live if you want it)

Staff photos by Jim Baird Richard Derk

The Stones bring crowd to its feet

Section AA, front row, center

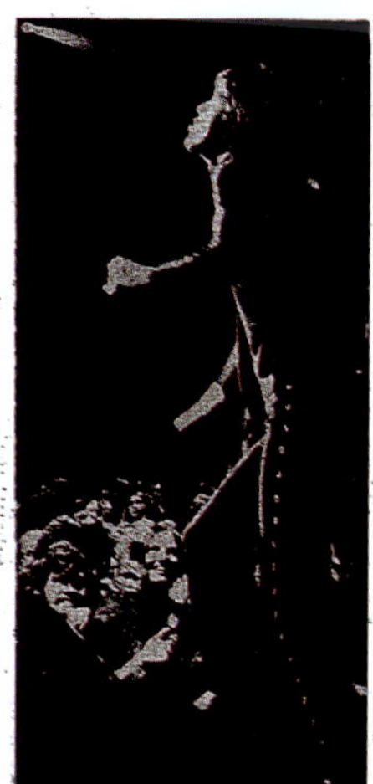

Working it out to 'Satisfaction'

Keith, Mick & Bill in action in Champaign, Illinois (Craig Petty)

TRIANGLE PRODUCTIONS INC.

THE ROLLING STONES

Plus TERRY REID and CHUCK BERRY

SUNDAY, NOVEMBER 16

2 Shows: 3 and 8 P.M.

INTERNATIONAL AMPHITHEATRE

\$6.50, \$5.50, \$4.50, \$3.50 \$2.50

TICKETS AVAILABLE AT BOX OFFICE AND ALL TICKETRON OU
Includ. MONTGOMERY WARD, MARSHALL FIELD and MET MUSIC ST

(clockwise from top left) Benjamin Krepak still has his free tour poster; Chicago show ad; Mark Thompson was third row centre in Chicago with his friend Harry; Raymond A Vanalot saw the Stones in Chicago; Mick performing 'Midnight Rambler' in Detroit (Katy MacLeod); Keith performing 'Prodigal Son' in Detroit (Katy MacLeod)

At the Spectrum

Rolling Stones Draw 14,279

By **JACK LLOYD**
Of The Inquirer Staff

It was like the good old days of rock 'n' roll, baby—the good old hysterical days when Elvis would shake his leg and the little girls went into orbit or a little later when the Beatles wore their hair like Prince Valiant and sang "It's Been A Hard Day's Night."

Except those were the innocent days, the pure, palmy days of rock music, when we were all a little younger and everything was a little less permissive.

Emotional expression came easier then. Vicarious sexual pleasure came with the twitch of a spasmic pelvis or a long undisciplined, anti-establishment lock of hair. And the little girls screamed and moaned.

MORE BLASE

There hasn't been much of that lately, because we are more blase than then. But the Rolling Stones brought it all back Tuesday night when these raucous tourists from England stopped by the Spectrum to pick up another installment on the roughly $2 million they will earn when their cross-country travels in the colonies come to a smashing finale later this week.

The little girls, of course, have graduated since those good old days. The vicarious thrills come harder now. It takes dirty talk, blatant symbolism, outrageous suggestion and the promise of sweet physical fulfillment.

It takes the Rolling Stones.

No, it takes Mick Jagger, because without Mick Jagger they would be just another outstanding rock group. It would not be the group that lured 14,279 into the Spectrum Tuesday night to constitute a sellout crowd that came to be turned on by that Rolling Stones brand of raw, no-holds-barred entertainment.

2D HOTTEST GROUP

With Mick Jagger, the Stones come out in the musical sweepstakes as the second hottest rock group in the world. No. 1, when you figure that the Beatles are not really a touring unit anymore.

It was a long night at the Spectrum.

First there were Terry Reid and B. B. King to warm the crowd up. And finally the Stones appeared at 11:15 P. M.

Jagger pranced around a bit and then the Stones broke into "Jumping Jack Flash."

Considering the Stones' reputation for tearing things up, it all started on a restrained note. The emotion was there, but it was simmering just beneath the surface.

The Stones then slowed things down even more with a blues number, "Love In Vain," from their new album. Then Jagger looked out over the huge crowd and said, "Welcome to my kitchen." He was obviously beginning to loosen up. By then the witching hour was near and so naturally these self-styled "devils' disciples" were starting to get with it.

The pace picked up quickly with "Midnight Rambler." The beat was hard, the rhythm pounded and Jagger's lyrics shot out like licks of brutal red-hot flames.

BUILT-UP STAGE

Once again Jagger strutted, danced, pranced, mugged and gyrated his hips, taunting his audience.

It was 12:05 A. M. Wednesday when the Stones tore into one of their biggest songs, "Satisfaction." Jagger chanted out the words—"I Can't Get No Satisfaction"—and that did it. Everyone in the Spectrum was on his feet, moving and clapping and shouting and screaming. Now the Stones were down to serious business and Jagger was going at top speed.

Yes, it was like the old days. Well, almost.

(clockwise from top left) Philly Spectrum review; Mick on stage in Boston (Linda Markham); Philly Spectrum advert; *Daily News* MSG review; tickets for Philly (Anthony Zumpano), Baltimore & MSG (Dari Silverman)

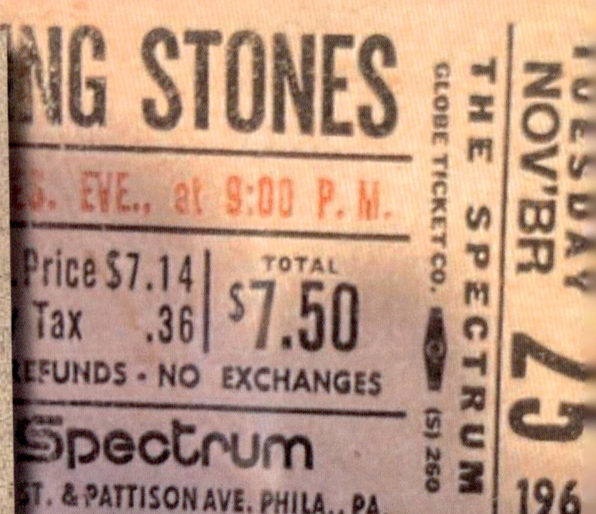

NOVEMBER 28, 1969

Lead singer Mick Jagger, a Rolling Stone who gathers no moss, turns on the fans at the Garden last night.

Jagger the Spectacular Blows 16,283 Minds

By JOHN QUINN

"The show is not the show but they that go," the poet Emily Dickinson wrote a long time ago.

Well, things haven't changed much to judge by the gaily-robed cast of 16,283 true believers who rocked along with Mick Jagger and the four other Rolling Stones at Madison Square Garden last night.

Sound and Spectacle

This first of three Stones' concerts (there's a matinee and another evening show tonight) was difficult to [illegible] submerged in the tumult of the crowd, however mightily the amplifiers tried to pierce it—and mightily did they try. (I have pierced eardrums to prove it.)

First, Hammer, Then the Dynamite

And in strictly musical terms, there's actually little to report other than the performance of Mick Taylor, the new guitarist, who replaces the late Brian Jones. Taylor looks like a cherub painted by Rubens, but plays a hard, gutty guitar that showed to splendid effect in a long, feral solo at the end of a new and faster arrangement of the Stones' popular "Sympathy for the Devil." He is a very accomplished

For the most part, the Stones adhered like cork plaster to the basic rock gospel: First hammer 'em into the ground, then dynamite them. With few variations, they played their familiar songs to the familiar beat with the familiar profane joy that is their musical cachet.

But pop music is as much spectacle as it is music (at its worst, more so, which is why some folk, wrongly, still dismiss the form). And Jagger is a spectacular showman.

He artfully escalated the crowd's response from enthusiasm to mania in just about an hour and a half, spitting out with customary slack-lipped

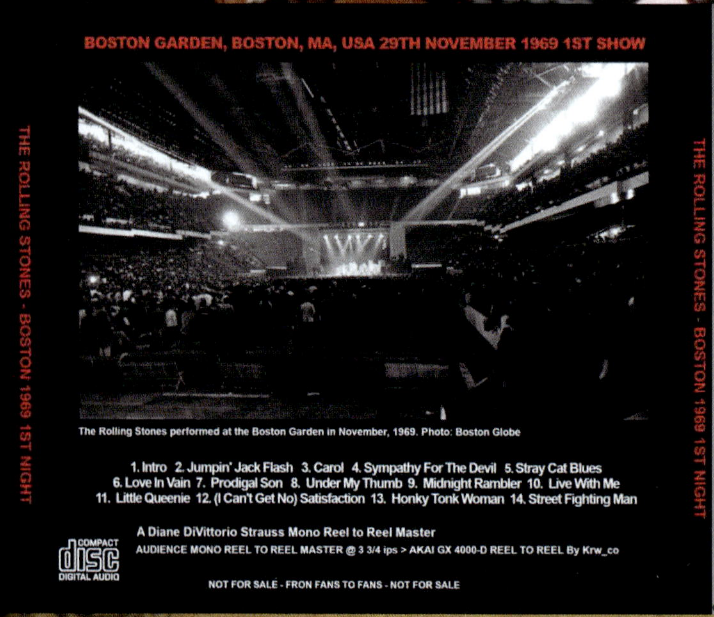

BOSTON GARDEN, BOSTON, MA, USA 29TH NOVEMBER 1969 1ST SHOW

THE ROLLING STONES - BOSTON 1969 1ST NIGHT

The Rolling Stones performed at the Boston Garden in November, 1969. Photo: Boston Globe

1. Intro 2. Jumpin' Jack Flash 3. Carol 4. Sympathy For The Devil 5. Stray Cat Blues 6. Love In Vain 7. Prodigal Son 8. Under My Thumb 9. Midnight Rambler 10. Live With Me 11. Little Queenie 12. (I Can't Get No) Satisfaction 13. Honky Tonk Woman 14. Street Fighting Man

A Diane DiVittorio Strauss Mono Reel to Reel Master

AUDIENCE MONO REEL TO REEL MASTER @ 3 3/4 ips > AKAI GX 4000-D REEL TO REEL By Krw_co

COMPACT disc DIGITAL AUDIO

NOT FOR SALE - FRON FANS TO FANS - NOT FOR SALE

THE ROLLING STONES - BOSTON 1969 1ST NIGHT

FIRST ANNUAL INTERNATION

FESTIVA

IRON BUTTERFLY • CANNED HEAT • SPOOKY

THE ROLLING STONES • JANIS JOPLIN • CH

BROS. • SLY & THE FAMILY STONE • JEF

AIRPLANE • THE BYRDS • STEPPENWOLF

• PACIFIC GAS & ELECTRIC • SWEETW

COUNTRY JOE & THE FISH • JOHNNY W

• ROTARY CONNECTION • GRAND FUNK RA

• THE RUGBYS • KING CRIMSON • PLUS 1

FAMOUS GROUPS • FOR INFO. CALL 305-

(clockwise from top) Altamor
(Steven Marcus); Palm Beach Festiv
poster; Joe & Cheryl Pruss dov
front at Altamont; Diane Strauss ge
a credit on the Boston bootle

The Rolling Stones tape an appearance for *The Ed Sullivan Show* performing 'Gimme Shelter' and closing the show with 'Love In Vain' and 'Honky Tonk Women'. While Mick Jagger sang live, the band mimed to pre-recorded tracks. Broadcast on 23 November, it was to be the band's sixth (and last) appearance on the show.

The band had considered appearing on *The Smothers Brothers* show but Sullivan had a bigger audience.

24 NOVEMBER 1969

DETROIT OLYMPIA
DETROIT
MICHIGAN

"Compared to the way we sounded later along, we were terrible in San Francisco. Ragged. By the time we were in Detroit, I'd say, it was like a one hundred percent improvement"

MICK JAGGER

JILL FARBER-BRAMSON

I was the little girl who started dancing in front of the black-and-white TV set with my big sister while watching *American Bandstand*. I was doing the Mashed Potato, Mess Around, Pony, Swim, Monkey and the Twist. I was also the wee child who had Beatlemania and loved the British Invasion.

In 1964 my dad dropped off my sister and I at the Olympia Stadium in Detroit, Michigan to see The Beatles, which was an experience I'll never forget. It was a thrilling frenzy of a sensational new sound and look mixed with a lot of screaming coming from a packed and euphoric audience of mostly girls and young women. When my dad picked us up afterwards, he could see that we were deliriously happy. I knew right then and there that there would be many more concerts in my life.

In 1969 I was a 15-year-old high school student who was brought up by liberal Democratic parents who were big on voting, civic involvement and the arts, including a diversity of music and nature. (I'm still devoted to all of the above.) While I was drawing and painting or just hanging out by myself or with my friends, I was listening to a wide variety of musical groups and bands, including the Rolling Stones. (Of course, years earlier, like millions of other American kids, I saw The Beatles as well as the Stones on *The Ed Sullivan Show.)* I remembered seeing Mick Jagger singing 'Satisfaction' and later on how there was a tug of war between the Stones and *The Ed Sullivan Show* over 'Let's Spend The Night Together' (and whether they would be allowed to sing the lyrics as recorded – they weren't). Of course, I loved 'Sympathy For The Devil', 'You Can't Always Get What You Want', 'Jumpin' Jack Flash', 'Street Fighting Man' and 'Mother's Little Helper'.

When I heard through one of the local radio stations, like WABX, that the Stones were coming to the Olympia, I asked my best friend at the time if she wanted to attend the concert. She said yes and that it would be so cool.

The venue was packed and I remember thinking that the room looked like an ocean of hair. We were all basically flower children and/or hippies. There were young people my age, but also young people in their late adolescence and older. There was the fragrance of pot in the air. A lot of people were stoned. (My friend and I were not.)

I remember some guys in their early twenties who were sitting near us wondering out loud if 'the girls are going to scream?'. I told them no. They liked that. And I was correct. There wasn't screaming, just a lot of cheering, swaying and dancing.

The audience members entertained themselves before the (so-called) warm up acts performed. Terry Reid rocked it. However, I was particularly delighted to hear

BB King play his guitar Lucille. I loved his brilliant blues.

When the Rolling Stones were announced the room of rockers went wild with yelling, screaming and applause and were jumping up and down. It was so loud and the energy and excitement were electrifying.

But the initial yelling and screaming quickly subsided because everyone wanted to hear every line of each song. Mick Jagger's bone-thin body was sheathed in an all black, clingy jumpsuit that he was gliding, sliding, slithering and almost flying around the stage in, while bending forward, at times, into the audience that was in a deliriously happy and euphoric frenzy. He was lightning fast and gyrating all over the place. The audience went particularly wild in a thrilling and joyful way when Mick took the extra, extra-long bright red scarf he had from around his neck and started softly 'beating' the audience with it.

As well as loving music and how it takes me to a different place through the beat, rhythm, tone, sound, pitch, volume, variety, continuity and lyrics, I also love how an emotion-charged, dramatic and exaggeratedly expressive performance makes me feel. From what I saw and was experiencing at Olympia that day, I could feel that everyone was rocking, rolling and vibrating with a unique kind of excitement from a rare musical experience that we almost couldn't believe was happening (to us).

My best friend and I would look at each other and smile, laughing uncontrollably and shaking our heads in disbelief while moving and dancing to the music. It was like a personal, communal happening we were sharing in a huge room with a bunch of strangers and we were all having a blast. It was an incredible experience. It was so cool!

JOHN ORLICH

I was just 17 and in a band, The Stuart Avery Assemblage (aka Assemblage). Our band was really into the Stones; they were like gods to us and we all went to the concert together. It's the only Stones concert I've ever been to. I remember asking my mom for the nine dollars for the ticket. That's all it cost, and we had tenth row seats on the main floor! We heard that the Stones got over $50,000 for that gig, and we were just blown away by that amount. This was the first tour with Mick Taylor on guitar and we were impressed by his playing but felt that, visually, he just was not a Stone. The Stones were incredible that night, very tight, and had great showmanship.

My band eventually cut an album and a single, a cover of 'Satisfaction'.

RICH DORRIS

I was 18 years old. It was five dollars to see any of the big bands in those days and I saw just about everyone but The Beatles! The Stones show was at the Olympia Stadium in Detroit. There were no seats. But my fondest memory of the Stones is riding shotgun in a red 1964 Plymouth Sport Fury convertible, bucket seats and all. It was my older brother's car and we must have stolen it as my sister was driving, me being underage. She 'laid rubber' and generally hot rodded with the top down through the streets of Detroit with 'Satisfaction' blasting out of the AM radio.

KATY MCLEOD

A week and a half later, I flew from Chicago to St Louis to pick up some friends and the four of us went to Detroit. We were on the stage in Detroit even though our seats were in the rafters, in the nosebleeds. We worked our way down to the front until our elbows were on the stage. The people in the row didn't seem to mind. It was another amazing show. I have a lot of pictures from Detroit. My friend went backstage again.

FRED YUCHT

It was the first of six times that I've seen the Stones. They've aways been the centre of my rock and roll experience, and my favourite band. Time has clouded my memory, but I remember rushing and getting to within about 15 feet of the stage. I'm confident I had direct eye contact with Bill Wyman for about ten seconds, or so it seemed. Their performance and music were great and they confirmed to me that they were the greatest rock and roll band. Their encore was 'Satisfaction' and it was a real treat seeing them.

DAVE MARSH, *CREEM*

Yes, indeed-dop-diddly-do the Rollfucking Stones – high energy superjamsters who played in my own home town at our very own ice hockey rink November 24th and were they good? You could say that... The Rolling Stones are back and they are the greatest band in the world and they really are the greatest they really are and they are back, the Rolling Stones are back and they really are the greatest goddamn band in the land... no shit.

UNCREDITED, *ANN ARBOR ARGUS*

So Mick Jagger, by all accounts a rather *bad* mothuhfuckuh, came home. Grotesque, lewd, and deranged. Satisfying.

Jagger's sassy strut and faggoty pirouettes, black leotards and black muscle shirt (his sun sign, Leo, in place of Superman 'S'), and a flippant red floor-length scarf decorate the heavy, hard-driving rock pulsar like lace draped over a lathe. Olympia Stadium's 15,000 rightful owners gape, scream, crawl up on the arms of their seats, dance, charge the stage, wave fists and other less organised clumps of fingers, and when Micky bawls we all bawl with him: 'I can't get nooo... SA... TIS... FAC... TION!'

Positively a fire hazard. Convulsions, spasms, fists – Jagger answers with an affected postnasal drip, belly shimmies, and a spine whose erectness he probably owes to his father Joe, a physical education teacher. It's no capital crime.

But Satan is barefoot, a homespun boy, society's child. He dances the disease which this place is. He's the total imposter. The last of the great movie queens. The last of the great white pricks. Wealthy – the tour will pay for two million-dollar bashes. Lazy, narcissistic, a good businessman – the boy next door. Satan is the boy next door – and the boy next door has made art out of indecent exposure. He lets it bleed and the slow songs crawl out almost menstrually. He beats it off and we all pound with him. Bad. Bad.

The performance is pure ritual. Jagger bounces around; he's effeminate. He's like a peacock, flinging and flapping his red scarf. The rhythms are hard, the music is tough and violent, but Jagger comes on soft and curvey. He projects the complete inversion of the Beatles' All-Amerikan Bungalow Bill. He's everyone's pervert, the King and the Queen.

And 'Satisfaction' does it all. Everyone surges forward, everyone leans toward the one figure illuminated in the darkness. The words say one thing, but the message is out of control. 'Satisfaction' feels good because it really says how really bad things are. There's no satisfaction in school, in bed, in the Army, on the job, in the movies. And the wild response of the crowd is the thing that proves that's true. The whole audience is moving heavy 'cause the song is something they can feel. Total revulsion at the death and sterility of bourgeois life and the demand for some way out. People gotta have satisfaction. People don't wait too long. People pick up guns. People smash states. People make the Revolution.

But that's not what happened at the end of the concert. In fact, the way Jagger put things together, it wouldn't have even fit very well. They finished their street-fighting song and left the stage. People shouted for more; but the Stones were gone for good. Everyone went home missing what might have been an appropriate ending. Mick Jagger's last song could have been 'Come together right now over me.' He'd drawn the sexual energies of a coliseum full of people into his parcel of flesh

– and the crowd, both male and female – seemed a lot more ready to come all over Mick Jagger than find their way to the discipline, modesty, and restraint needed to make a real Revolution. A decadent air hung over the Stadium.

And our current level of struggle – clapping hands, cutting up, busting loose, fucking, blowing weed, and breaking windows – is a far cry from seizing state power. The Vietnam war drags on. We aren't half as miserable as most of the world. And a lot of the Revolution so far is just a hip ego trip. What do groupies, pimps, PR men, and ticket-takers have to do with the Revolution? Mick Jagger is still our wet dream, our illusion of release, a half-assed male-chauvinist prick, not a stone communist revolutionary.

MIKE GORMLEY, *DETROIT FREE PRESS*

Olympia estimates the crowd at 14,358 who watched BB King, Terry Reid and the Rolling Stones. Terry Reid and BB King would have been a show in itself. Both were very good, especially BB King, who threw in his comedy as well as the fantastic blues he's able to get out of Lucille, his guitar.

Roughly ten minutes after BB left the stage, Mick Jagger and the Stones presented themselves to the crowd. Jagger walked on stage wearing a black t-shirt with an omega insignia on his chest and black, tight pants with a large silver belt separating the two. On his head he had an Uncle Sam top hat. Around his neck was a red silk scarf hanging down below his knees. The Stones ran through old and new tunes, many of them from their new album *Let It Bleed*, while Mick danced and jumped his way around the stage. He stuck his tongue out at the crowd, then smiled at them, then sneered. His arms flew in the air, wild, then graceful, then dead as his feet took over and carried him to one corner of the stage then to the other.

The Stones seemed to be loving the whole thing, frequently smiling at each other, as if there was an inside joke making the rounds. Except for Jagger, The Rolling Stones were almost dead-pan. Bill Wyman on bass looked bored. Keith Richard, thin and wearing one earring swung back and forth a little. Charlie Watts on drums just beat as hard as he could and the new Stone. Mick Taylor simply played the guitar and enjoyed the show. They played good rock 'n' roll and Jagger gained points as the showman of the year.

25 NOVEMBER 1969

THE SPECTRUM SPORTS ARENA
PHILADELPHIA
PENNSYLVANIA

"Mick was in his Uncle Sam hat and charged into 'Jumpin' Jack Flash'"

ANTHONY ZUMPANO

ANTHONY ZUMPANO

I was 17 years old and a senior in high school in a suburb of Philadelphia. I found out that the Stones were coming to Philly and initially were going to do two shows on the same day – a matinee and evening performance. I bought tickets for the afternoon show and was excited to be going as I had been a fan since 1965 but had never seen them live. Unfortunately, the matinee show got cancelled and I was upset as the evening show was sold out. But I checked out a famous ticket agency in Philly named Glassmans and they still had tickets for sale! I bought two for the evening show and was pumped again about seeing the Stones live.

I had been driving for about a year and me a high school buddy drove to the Spectrum in Philadelphia that November night. When I got there, I found that our seats were on the side lower level, on the Mick Taylor side, and we had a great sight line to the stage.

Terry Reid was the opening act and did about 30 minutes as a three-piece group. I had never heard of him but enjoyed his music. Next up was BB King with his full orchestra and he was the real thing regarding the blues.

After his performance we waited until a local Philly DJ came on the stage and introduced the Stones; there was no Sam Cutler intro like in most cities. They hit the stage and Mick was in his Uncle Sam hat and charged into 'Jumpin' Jack Flash'. The sound of that band was phenomenal and I was in awe.

Jagger never stopped moving and Keith was slashing away on the riffs. 'Carol' came next and then 'Sympathy For The Devil'. Mick took this to another level and the duelling guitar solos between Taylor and Richards was incredible. The two acoustic songs were cool and intimate for a building like the Spectrum. The show went on, with Keith building momentum with the set list. When they got to 'Honky Tonk Women' the house lights went on and you could see everyone on their feet singing and dancing. Onto the last song, 'Street Fighting Man', and – bang – it was over with no encore.

I was transformed, as I had just witnessed the greatest rock and roll band in the world. After that show, I saw the Stones on every tour that came to Philly but nothing can top that first experience of the Stones and that iteration of the band. Charlie was good tonight!

STEVE CURSON

Me and a bunch of my friends went. One had a portable cassette recorder with which he taped the show. He has since passed away and I have no idea what happened to the tape. The funny part was him interviewing us before the show and one of us saying that we couldn't wait for Ike and Tina Turner to come on, which we did to piss off the one hardcore Stones fan in our group.

We also went up to Madison Square Garden and saw them there.

DAVE DARTNELL

A good friend of mine said there was no barrier between the seats and the stage and he got upfront and had his hands on the stage and Mick danced on his fingers. He said it hurt but he didn't care.

I wasn't allowed to go since I was only ten years old. I had to wait until they came back to the Spectrum in 1975. Since then, I have seen them 24 more times including once in England. In June 2024 they were back in Philly. It was my twenty-sixth time.

GEORGE KEAHEY

I remember going to see them with a friend's older brother in 1969. When I went again in 1972, I went to both shows as that older brother informed me that you needed to go to all the shows, because they'd play different songs at each.

LINDA ESRICH MATTISON

I was beyond dazzled by what was my first of seven Stones concerts. I distinctly recall Mick beating the stage with his wide belt during 'Midnight Rambler'.

MARIA MAGGIO

It was my fourteenth birthday. My father bought an entire row of seats for my friends (and my younger brothers) and me… The third row from the stage. Everyone rushed the stage and my father was telling us to sit down so we wouldn't get thrown to the floor. Naturally nobody did that. He asked the usher to have the lights turned on so he could see us and was told that couldn't be done. After some strong and meaningful threats, the overhead lights went on, he made sure we were okay and then the lights were turned off again. He went to one of the boxes and we enjoyed the concert! My dad called them 'The Rolling Rocks'…

TOM FARLEY

The preceding August I had gone with my friend Norm to the Atlantic City Pop Festival, which was a Woodstock preview – many of the same artists were on the same bill. In September we were at the original Electric Factory to see The Who, who were great. When they announced that the Stones would be on in November and that tickets would be nine dollars I was stunned. The Atlantic City Pop Festival had only cost $25 for a whole three days!

In those three months I got to see some of the greatest acts of that era. Seeing the Stones and these other great bands was the greatest eye (and ear) opener. We saw everyone who came through Philly, especially British groups, for the following 50-plus years. The anticipation of that night for the Stones was palpable, the crowd went wild when they started and they carried the crowd until the end. It was great.

I've seen every one of their Philadelphia shows since.

DAVID PRICE

It's so cliched to say that February 9, 1964 changed my life but it certainly put me on the path that led me through my life. I'm an only child and I remember sitting there watching this thing on CBS with my parents. My father was horrified because 'what the hell was this?' But my mother played piano and organ and had played music in church. She sensed something was there. I was just going, 'Wow, there's girls and they're screaming. Oh my God, what's that?' I was twelve years old.

Next day on the school bus, three things were happening. The girls were already writing the name of the Beatle they were going to marry on their notebooks (and poor Ringo was coming in a distant fourth). The boys were all saying, 'Oh, those faggots with long hair,' and, 'British this, that and the other.' And a small group of us were saying, 'Girls!'

I lived about an hour and five minutes from Atlantic City, home to Steel Pier. My parents would let me go and spend the whole day there, which I could do for something like $2.50. The first concert I ever saw was there in August 1965: Herman's Hermits. It was standing room only and I could only see maybe a quarter of the ballroom, but I counted 17 girls and one guy fainting. It was only later that I understood what the girls had already figured out; if you fainted you were taken backstage and might meet Peter Noone.

In 1966, I started playing keyboards. It was a Farfisa Mini Compact, the cheapest keyboard made – a harmonica on stilts – and I might be the only person in the world who had one of those and a Gibson Explorer amp.

The first real concert I ever went to was at the Convention Hall in Philly. My dad took me, the guitar player and the drummer in the band. The opening act was the Blues Magoos. They were into psychedelic lighting, and part of their light show was wrapping Christmas lights around their jackets. The next band was The Who, in their peak period of destroying everything available. And the last band was… Herman's Hermits. I hated Herman's Hermits. Was Peter Noone following me?

In the fall I enrolled at Villanova University, right outside of Philadelphia. My roommate and I lived off campus. We both liked music and I liked the Stones' music and their attitude. Villanova was on the main line into Philly. There was an elevated train that turned into a subway, so when the tour was announced my roommate and I went down to the box office at the Spectrum to get tickets. We paid something like $6.50, which was outrageous because that summer I had paid just three dollars to see ten bands at the Atlantic City Pop Festival. So the first thing that struck me about Stones tickets in 1969 was, 'Gee, this is a lot of money.'

Terry Reid opened, and very few people knew who Terry Reid was. I was almost as excited to see BB King as I was to see the Stones because I was a huge blues fan. The Stones came out and opened with 'Jumpin' Jack Flash'. I never really liked that song but the live version is much harder, much more rock, than the original recording with its acoustic guitar.

I was fascinated by the crowd because America back then – like we are now – was splitting into two groups of young people: those who looked at the Stones as something more than music and the pop fans who saw them as somebody who played *Ed Sullivan*. The original lyric in 'Sympathy For The Devil' was, 'Who killed John Kennedy?' and then, while they were in the studio, Robert Kennedy gets killed, and so it became, 'Who killed the Kennedys?' So you had the 'Satisfaction' crowd versus the 'Sympathy For The Devil' crowd.

Underground radio, FM radio, had come out in San Francisco in '67 and by '69 had moved to Philadelphia. The Stones were one of the few bands at that time that were played both on AM and FM radio.

I remember them playing an extended version of 'Midnight Rambler', and 'Carol' and 'Sympathy For The Devil'. You couldn't reproduce the opening to 'Sympathy' back then. Charlie Watts wasn't gonna get up and play bongos.

THE ROLLING STONES 1969 TOUR

26 NOVEMBER 1969

RAINBOW GRILL
ROCKEFELLER CENTER
NEW YORK
NEW YORK

"This is like being in the front row of a concert, like Philadelphia"

MICK JAGGER

The Stones host the only official press conference of the tour at the Rainbow Grill in Rockefeller Center. They are scheduled to play the Civic Center in Baltimore 200 miles away later that day.

THOM LUKAS

1969 was an exciting time to be able to see the Stones again, finally. And I wanted to get as close as I could to my favourite band in the world. But little did I know how close I would actually get.

The Rolling Stones had not toured America in about three years; just like The Beatles, they had stopped touring in late 1966. They may have done an *Ed Sullivan Show* in 1967, but they did not do an actual tour. This was their first time back and their first time with their new guitarist, who joined about five months before, Mick Taylor. Brian Jones had died right after being ousted from the Stones in favour of Taylor.

I was a huge fan of the band, having seen them twice in 1964. I had been reading with interest about the tour and how it had been going, and Nancy and I were lucky enough to be able to get some tickets for the Madison Square Garden Thanksgiving Day show because a friend of ours had waited on line outside in the cold overnight.

We got tickets for the Thanksgiving evening show; and tickets sold out so quickly that they added an afternoon show the following day. The opening bands were Terry Reid, BB King, and the Ike and Tina Turner Revue.

I read in the newspapers the day before the show, that the Stones would come to town and do a press conference in Rockefeller Center, at the top of the NBC building, in the Rainbow Room Grill. It was an exclusive place.

My friend Kevin and I decided to take off from school and go to the NBC building and see if we could sneak in somehow to this press conference. We were hoping it might be possible!

We got there about an hour or so before the press conference was scheduled to begin, and the lobby was crowded with obvious Rolling Stones fans standing near a side door. All of a sudden, some television lights went on, pointing toward that door, and that's when we realised that the Stones were entering the building.

The Stones arrived from a different entrance two minutes after Kevin and I got there: there was a cordon of security around them and they were being pushed slowly towards the elevator bank. I went to the elevator bank, because I knew they were going to be there in a few seconds. The Stones were shoved towards the elevator, the elevator door opened, and somehow I got pushed onto the elevator:

they had mistaken me, I realised later, for the new guitarist Mick Taylor! I had similar colour hair, similar length of hair, and I was young – about seventeen – while Mick Taylor was about four years older than me.

I'm forced onto the elevator, in the back; the Stones are around me on three sides, facing forward, and there's a bodyguard by the door, pushing the buttons. They all breathed a sigh of relief as soon as the heavy elevator door finally closed, there were smiles on their faces, like, 'We survived that!'

Then immediately we heard a pounding, a kind of a ferocious pounding on the elevator door, and they all looked worried. They all looked around and they realised that Mick Taylor was not there! There's this other guy there – me! They tell the bodyguard to open the elevator and Mick Taylor gets propelled into the elevator. He does not look so happy, but the other band members are cracking up! They think this is the funniest thing in the world.

While I am in awe of everything, I realise the bodyguard is glaring at me: he made a mistake, he let me in the elevator instead of Mick Taylor, he might lose his job or get in trouble because of this. So, he looks at me and says, 'When this elevator stops, you better stay on this elevator.' I took that to mean that I was in the doghouse, that I was in trouble and this was not a party. I kind of slunk even more to the back, trying to avoid eye contact with anybody in the group and trying to make myself invisible.

The Rainbow Room is on the sixty-fifth floor of the NBC building, and that was quite a ride, especially with those slow elevators from the thirties and forties that had not really been upgraded, so it seemed as if the elevator ride was taking a long time and I did not feel comfortable.

The Stones eventually settled down, Taylor lost the funk that he was in from being locked out of the elevator and they all started talking to each other in hushed voices.

Mick and Keith were whispering to each other in the front, Charlie and Bill were whispering to each other, closer to me, and Mick Taylor, near the bodyguard, was on his own, like me. I was crouched down in the back, not giving anybody eye contact after that glare I got from the bodyguard. I could see the clothes that Charlie and Bill were wearing, and I could see the fact that they had pancake make-up on; I had never seen any male wearing make-up. Obviously, it was because of the lights of the cameras at the press conference they were going to, so it didn't seem too weird. I remember Charlie was wearing a tan/grey leather jacket. I was so close to that jacket I was studying the details of it; it looked like high quality, soft leather. I couldn't make out clearly what everybody was saying, but they were talking like friends. It was a long elevator ride.

When we finally got to the sixty-fifth floor the bodyguard reminded me, 'You better stay on this elevator.' They all quickly got off, and I felt relieved: 'Wow, I'm free. I'm not part of this crazy scene anymore,' this high tension, paranoid thing that was show business.

Then suddenly, I saw Keith Richards, wearing a dark velvet jacket, returning to the still-open door of the elevator, looking right at me! He crouched down, stuck his finger out like it was a gun and said, 'Okay, you STAY on this elevator!' like he was threatening me, but then he smiled and waved goodbye, and was off to his press conference.

The door closed and I went all the way down and told my friend Kevin what happened. Neither one of us could believe what had just taken place. We would watch the press conference on the TV news later that evening. That's the one where a reporter asks if Mick Jagger is more satisfied now with his life, referring of course to the song 'Satisfaction,' and Mick says something about being satisfied sexually, but not financially.

When I stared in a mirror, I still couldn't see any similarity to Mick Taylor; I was trying to look like Alvin Lee, because he was my hero at that point. That day I became Mick Taylor for ten minutes – it was the longest ten minutes of my life.

THE WASHINGTON POST

After being submitted to a security check unrivalled at the Pentagon, journalists were given drinks and canapés while a string quartet played Haydn.

In contrast to how the Stones had been depicted in the media for the previous five years, the AP report said that the Stones were 'the most polite persons there.' There was pandemonium among the press trying to get their questions in, leading Jagger to ask, 'Shall we scream at you like you're screaming at us?' Jagger was also asked his opinion of New York City, to which he responded, 'It's great. It changes. It explodes.' He was also asked if he had yet felt satisfied, to which he responded, 'Financially dissatisfied, sexually satisfied, philosophically trying.'

The most notable thing to come out of the press conference was the announcement that the group would be headlining a daylong free concert in Golden Gate Park in San Francisco, though the group also shot down longstanding rumours that they would do a similar free show in Central Park. ('Now is too cold,' Jagger said. 'We've got to do it outside. And San Francisco is really into that sort of thing.')

26 NOVEMBER 1969

CIVIC CENTER
BALTIMORE
MARYLAND

"It was so long ago and yet just thinking about it and remembering makes it seem closer"

LYNN LAGERSTROM

"I got my eyes on you sugar 'cos you dance so good..."

MICK JAGGER

ALLAN SPRECHER

There were four of us, all 17. We scrounged tickets costing $8.50 apiece at the last minute. In those days you were in one of two camps. Either The Beatles, the popular acceptable long-haired magical music makers, or the demonic, edgy, naughty, 'don't let your daughter near those guys' Rolling Stones. We were going to see the Rolling Stones!

By the time we got to our seats, lower mezzanine, left of the stage, we were in a cloud of excitement. The constant din of noise was proof that something was about to happen. Everyone was anxious and waiting for the show to begin.

The lights lowered, and the Terry Reid Band took the stage. Bang bang! And then the big man with Lucille, BB King. The thrill was not gone, but gaining momentum. We were here to see the Rolling Stones!

It was a small eternity between acts. The Stones were running late. The anticipation, excitement and noise were building to a crescendo. The lights lowered, the spot light hit the stage, and…

'Ladies and Gentlemen, THE ROLLING STONES!'

The crowd went wild! Mick was dressed in black with the Greek letter Omega on a long sleeve t-shirt with little metal symbols that ran down the outside seams of his trousers. He was wearing a long scarf and an Uncle Sam top hat. Everyone was on their feet moving forward, with everyone jammed as close as possible to the stage to experience every ounce of the aura and to behold the Rolling Stones!

Magically, and without recollection, they materialised at the front of the stage: Mick Jagger, Mick Taylor, Keith Richards, Charlie Watts and Bill Wyman. The first ripping notes of 'Jumpin' Jack Flash' rang out and the charge was detonated. The crowd – cheering, singing, yelling, laughing, crying – was amazing. The noise decibels were off the chart. The band rocked on with Mick swirling, jaunting, taunting, jumping and banging his tambourine. This is what we all came to witness.

Between songs Mick addressed the audience. I really couldn't hear what he was saying because everyone was yelling, 'Mick! Mick! Mick!' from all directions.

Then there was dead silence, for a nano second, nothingness. A fluke in time where everything stopped, frozen animation, the pause button was pushed.

Being a garage band bass player with 'Satisfaction' and 'Under My Thumb' as part of our repertoire, I was and am a big Bill Wyman fan. I was at the front of the stage looking up at Bill and I yelled, 'Bill!' He was looking out at the crowd and then looked down and I gave him the 'OK' hand sign, thumb and index finger together to form an O. With his left hand holding the guitar neck and his right hand resting on the body of the guitar, he acknowledged me with a slight raising of his fingers. His thumb still resting on the guitar, he gave me a little wave. A smile.

In a wink the band were into their next number. The crowd noise was as though the pause button had never been hit. The guitarists were hitting their stride and Charlie's drums were banging out an intoxicating rhythm. The crowd reaction was once again off the chart.

Wow! On this Thanksgiving Eve 1969, we were part of the audience that came to experience one of the greatest! Ladies and gentlemen, the Rolling Stones!

JANATHAN BROWN

I think seats were $5.00 down stairs and $2.50 balcony. I had just started see someone. I had already had seats for the show. So I don't know how, but he snuck in, probably during intermission. I love the Stones, but I only got to see half of the show because he and I went into the balcony and made out for the rest of the show . I still love the Stones. I would have gone into the balcony with Mick if he had only asked me!

JON SEIFF, AGE 17

The opening acts were Terry Reid and BB King. Tickets were $7.50 but I got one for five dollars as a friend couldn't get a date (for the Stones!) so I tagged along. It was an amazing show. I believe one or two songs from this show ended up on *Get Your Ya-Ya's Out*.

LYNN LAGERSTROM

I saw the Stones on their 1969 tour on Thanksgiving night. I remember being so excited and looking forward to it. The show was in the Garden, of course, and as I recall it was a good one. Jagger was at his peak because I believe it was towards the end of the tour and I also think it was Mick Taylor's first tour with them. Ike and Tina Turner opened but I was so excited about the Stones I don't remember much about their performance and I could kick myself because I'm sure they were as explosive as they always were. God, it was so long ago and yet just thinking about it and remembering makes it seem closer. It was a great show and a good time. Later on, I heard that Jimi Hendrix was at the show too but I don't recall seeing him perform so maybe he was just there to watch the show. I just feel so blessed and lucky to have been born in this era – the best music ever!

27 NOVEMBER 1969

MADISON SQUARE GARDEN
NEW YORK
NEW YORK

"In all the future gigs, we want to keep the audiences as a small as possible. We'd rather play to four shows of 5,000 people each, than one mammoth 50,000 sort of number... We're playing at Madison Square Garden in New York, but it will be a reduced audience, because we're not going to allow them to sell all the seats"

KEITH RICHARDS

"Ahh, New York City, ya talk a lot, let's have a look atcha"

MICK JAGGER

CAROL SIEGEL

This was the first of three shows they played at Madison Square Garden. Opening for the Stones were Terry Reid, BB King and the Ike and Tina Turner Revue. Janis Joplin sang with Tina. Jimi Hendrix sat on the side of the stage. This was Thanksgiving night. I never went to my loge seat. I squeezed into the first row along with a hundred others.

CATHY MARINO-FOY

The energy in the audience was kinetic. No one was sitting in their seats, that's for sure. It started with Ike and Tina Turner performing 'Proud Mary' and continued through the entire Stones set, with Mick strutting the stage with this red feather boa scarf, tight low riding pants and the audience screaming for more. Who was I with? Well, this is up for debate, as the person I would have sworn I was with recently told me he was not there! I was just 17 at the time. I became a fan from the first time I heard 'Satisfaction'. I loved their bluesy black sound and bad boy attitude, which was so different from The Beatles. The '69 tour was my first opportunity to see them, and it so entranced me that I've stayed a fan ever since.

JOHN ANDREWS

I saw the Stones three times on the '69 tour. I had long been a fan and had their early albums in high school: *12x5*, *Out Of Our Heads*, *High Tides... Beggar's Banquet* is my favourite, and *Let It Bleed* is probably next.

I was enrolled at the University of Illinois but missed their performance there because I was back in Washington at an anti-war demonstration. But my best friend, Robert, and I went to the show in Philly, then MSG and then Boston Garden.

MSG was the most memorable. During the opening acts, Robert and I were roaming around the arena. BB King opened all three shows at MSG, and then Ike and Tina Turner, who had the place hopping. When Janis Joplin jumped on stage and started a duet with Tina, the place went so berserk they literally had to pull the plug. And it wasn't just a switch flip. They cut the power. All the red lights on the amps on stage went out. It was pitch black until things settled down.

Back then, concert security was not like it is today. As we got near the Stones taking the stage, Robert and I positioned ourselves to rush the stage. We and a bunch of others bowled through the Andy Frain ushers and got right in front of the stage. We catapulted a couple of willing girls onto the stage so we could get closer. We got right in front of the stage with no one in front of us for most of the show. I remember Mick drank some Coke, and I said, 'Boo! Coke!' He heard me and said something (but I don't remember what).

I was 19 at the time, Robert 18. A friend of ours who was a film student worked for the Maysles on the edit for *Gimme Shelter*. He told us that hundreds of feet of film featuring Robert and me were left on the cutting room floor. I haven't looked lately, but there is about eight seconds of me in front of the stage with a girl on my shoulder.

I don't really remember much about the Philly show except we started out in the nosebleed seats and worked our way forward. Boston Garden I mostly remember because my little brother went with us. He was 14 at the time.

And I had tickets for the '72 tour but wound up in the hospital with an injury and had to bag out. I don't think I have seen them since.

RICH TROTTO

It was an amazing night. Terry Reid opened, who was probably not well known to many who attended that night, but he was very well known as an exciting guitarist and performer to those of us who saw his frequent appearances opening for more well-known groups at the Filmore East. He was followed by BB King, who was about a polished guitarist and performer as you can get. He delivered a strong set and then he was followed by Ike and Tina Turner, who blew the roof off the place.

The Stones seemed a little rough following BB King and then Ike and Tina, but that didn't last long. They really gelled on 'Sympathy For The Devil', and after that they tore the place up. The other song that I remember being a standout, over 50 years later, is 'Midnight Rambler'.

SAM SILBERSTEIN

My Brooklyn NY crowd used to argue about their favourite groups but one always said it was the Stones that were the best. He was a fan since 'Satisfaction' in 1965. When the '69 tour of America was announced and Madison Square Garden tickets went on sale, he cashed his paycheck and bought us all Stones tickets. He said, 'Now I'll prove it to you guys. When you see the Stones live, you will all agree with me.'

It was Thanksgiving weekend, November 1969 at MSG, and we go to see 'the greatest rock 'n' roll band in the world… the Rolling Stones!' Across the aisle from me was a teeny-bopper (she didn't look more than 14 or 15) who told me, 'And tomorrow I'm sitting over there and then over there…' as she pointed out her seats for the other shows she was going to see. Meanwhile I'm thinking, 'Who goes to see the same show again and again?' Besides, we all thought the prices were a rip-off at eight dollars a ticket. We went to the Fillmore East for four or five bucks!

Well, by the time we were walking out I was saying, 'Why aren't I going to the next two shows? I want more Stones!'

STEVE HAZE

Me and a few friends went down to the venue. A friend brought a tyre iron and popped open a door and we all ran in just as the Stones came on and I heard Jagger say something about his trousers…

28 NOVEMBER 1969

MADISON SQUARE GARDEN
NEW YORK
NEW YORK

BABA LOU

I was at the (late) Thanksgiving show in 1969 at Madison Square Garden.

I was never a Beatles fan. I was more into the Kinks and the Animals. When *High Tide and Green Grass* came out, I listened to my friend's copy of it and discovered many songs that NYC Top 20 radio stations didn't play due to the constant playing (and replaying) of Beatles records. I then got *12x5* and *December's Children* and was hooked. My favourite songs were 'Tell Me', 'Heart Of Stone', As Tears Go By', 'Congratulations' and then 'Time Is On My Side'.

By now, I was 15. I always wanted to be a drummer until Brian and Keith rocked the guitar and then I bought a cheap rhythm line electric with one pick up. I learned as many Stones songs as I could but my talent was limited. Then lightning struck as each LP got better – *Got Live If You Want It!*, *Aftermath*, *Between The Buttons*, *Flowers and Beggar's Banquet*. By then my childhood sweetheart and I needed to see a live show…

So in November of 1969 it was announced that the Stones would do three shows: Thanksgiving Eve, an early Thanksgiving show and the 8pm show, which we attended.

The opening act was Terry Reid, then BB King. Next up was the Ike and Tina Turner Revue. Their last song was 'Proud Mary' and Janis Joplin climbed up on the stage and joined in. In the audience was Sly Stone and backstage Jimi Hendrix was peeking his head out. At least, that was the talk in the stands.

After a 40-minute pause, out strutted Mick in his black outfit with a horseshoe symbol on the shirt. He was wearing a top hat and cape. The crowd was in a frenzy as Mick and company rocked the house. During this time, he paused and stated that he had popped a button on his trousers. He remarked, 'You don't want my trousers to fall down now, do you?' The crowd went wild. They did songs from *Beggar's Banquet* including an acoustic 'Prodigal Son' with Keith. 'Love In Vain' was when Mick introduced Mick Taylor, who played amazing slide guitar, They rocked with 'Carol', 'Stray Cat Blues', 'Sympathy For The Devil', 'Jumpin' Jack Flash', 'Street Fighting Man', 'Midnight Rambler' (as he whipped the stage with his belt), and an encore of 'Satisfaction'. It truly was a magical night.

My fiancée is now my wife of 50 years. We have seen them in every decade since. Our last show was in 2022, sadly without Charlie. Our wedding song in 1973 was 'Let's Spend The Night Together'.

NATALIE HAYES

I was 18 and went with my cousin to the late show. We didn't have tickets but managed to get some for $8. It was fantastic, especially 'Midnight Rambler'! He would slam his belt on the floor during the song. It didn't finish until after midnight. I had an awesome time!

THOM LUKAS

The Madison Square Garden show the night after the press conference was a little bit disappointing, one reason being Brian Jones' absence. Also I couldn't get as close as I wanted to, and to cap it off, I didn't have my usual telephoto lens because I was using a new camera. To make the experience even worse, the crowd was pushing forward, and… I got shoved into Grace Slick! She turned around and gave me an icy cold look. She realised, however, it wasn't me that was groping her, it was just me being pushed by the crowd. She was wearing a light colour fur coat, and it was coincidental that we had both been at Bill Graham's Thanksgiving party at the Fillmore East earlier that same afternoon. Another coincidence was that Janis Joplin, who also was at Bill Graham's party earlier that day (and who gave me a lusty look!), joined Ike and Tina Turner on stage for one song when they did their set

During one of several intermissions between bands, Nancy and I went into the area where people were buying snacks and beverages, and by chance, met with John Chappina, a photographer that I knew from the Fillmore East, and I asked him to take a photo, with my camera, of Nancy and I posed underneath a light. That kind of documents the night for me.

TOM GOULD

In 1969, the only way to buy tickets to concerts was exclusively at the box office. With my father working in Manhattan, he was able to stop by the Madison Square Garden box office on his way to Penn Station to catch his train home on the Long Island Railroad. He bought three tickets to see the Rolling Stones.

I was 16 at the time and my brothers were four and six years older than me. Our age difference meant that my brothers were firmly ensconced in the folk music genre while I was the only rock and roller in the family. They were enlisted to take me to the show.

My brothers were sporting jackets and ties. I was not wearing a tie. Before the show started, I spotted a familiar figure just a couple of sections away. It was Bob Dylan. I turned to my brother Rick and asked to borrow a cigarette. I took it and went down to the section where Dylan was sitting. I went up to the guy sitting next to Dylan and asked for a light for my cigarette. After lighting the cigarette, I stood up and looked right at Dylan. I said to him, 'I thought I heard that you were in New York. Are you John Lennon?' He looked at me and said 'yes'. We both smiled and I went on my way.

Soon after I returned to my seat, I noticed that a crowd had formed around Dylan and he had to move away from there.

It was a great concert. Google says that Terry Reid opened the show, but I have no recollection of him. I clearly remember seeing BB King playing the blues on his guitar, Lucille. Ike and Tina Turner turned up the heat with a high energy set featuring the dazzling Ikettes.

The Stones commanded the stage and easily held their own side by side with the other legendary performers. Brian Jones had left the band and then died by July of that year. This show featured Mick Taylor, new to the band. He played great.

DARI SILVERMAN

I was home from college for Thanksgiving in November of 1969. Usually I didn't bother, since it's a short break and I was at a university about 400 miles away. But this was going to be one of the last Thanksgivings ever with our whole family. My parents were going to move to the dreaded state of Florida from New York and my older brother had gotten married and was moving to Washington DC. So it was that I had zero excuse for not being at our traditional holiday dinner. Luckily for me, my friend Larry was also away at school across the country in Oregon, some 2,500 miles away. I say 'lucky' because he had two floor tickets for the Friday after Thanksgiving matinee show for the Rolling Stones at Madison Square Garden and he was giving me one of them.

Now, here's the thing. It's hard to imagine for me today, but I hadn't seen the Stones in concert before. They had played NYC three times before 1969 and I could have gone to any of those shows… but didn't. Back when you were a teen, it became, 'Are you a Stones fan or are you a Beatles fan?' The print media had set up the rivalry which, of course, sold magazines. At 14 or 15 years old, it became about loyalty and I was a loyal Beatles fan.

That never stopped me from buying the Stones records or loving their music. I was even a huge closet Brian Jones fan, so when he died in 1969 right before they came to America in 1969, I thought, 'Enough is enough. I have to be there.'

I had no idea who I was going to be sitting with. The other ticket was being taken by another friend of Larry's. Larry was cool, he was lead guitarist in a band, we were definitely into the same music. Naturally, I assumed his friend would also be fun to hang out with.

Unfortunately, he was as animated as wallpaper. I learned this when Terry Reid came out to open the show. This guy sat through the whole set, but a lot of people did. Sadly, I don't remember much about Terry's set but he was an amazing guitarist. When you're waiting to see the Stones for the first time, everyone's an 'also ran'. That would all change when the Ike and Tina Turner Revue hit the stage. Anyone who had the ability to sit through that set was either comatose or dead, as far as I was concerned. My seat mate was definitely one or the other. Without a doubt, Tina blew everyone in that audience away.

It's easy now to turn on YouTube and see what it was like to watch that much energy explode across the screen. However, seeing it up close and right in front of you, back when the internet didn't exist, was a whole other story. It's also hard to understand now, but it was not the thing in the mid-sixties for any female singer to be that sexual and that animated on stage. I'd seen every great girl group from earlier in the decade – The Chantelles, The Shirelles, The Ronettes and The Supremes – and they all sounded great, but Tina was a whole other species of woman/entertainer. I was devastated to learn that the night before, Thanksgiving night, while my family was eating dinner, Janis Joplin had joined Tina onstage for that night's show. Two of the most talented explosive women in music together at the microphone, and me eating turkey not that far away and missing it all.

During the break, after Tina and the Ikettes left the stage, it was hard to imagine that the Stones would top what I had just seen. How did they even let any group that dynamic open for them? It's a tribute to the Stones that both on this tour and on their 1972 tour, with Stevie Wonder opening, they had bands who rivalled them in terms of both talent and stage presence. On the other hand, it's a smart move to get your audience on their feet, already pumped and ready for more. We were ready... and so were they.

Tina had absolutely ruled that stage and Mick started out looking like a cheap imitation of her at the beginning of the show. But by the next couple of songs, he absolutely came into his own. It hurt me not to see Brian up there on stage, but this was Mick and the band in their prime, in their element. From the opening notes of 'Jumpin' Jack Flash' through 'Stray Cat Blues' (still one of my favourite lesser-celebrated songs) to my ultimate favourite of that time, 'Under My Thumb' (screw politically correct; I'm a feminist but this is rock and roll!) to Mick stalking that stage like a demon during 'Sympathy For The Devil', they lived up to my highest expectations.

My younger brother had seen them in Hyde Park during that summer in 1969. I have to say that the first time I saw this on video, I realised how much better it was to see this concert inside, in the proper setting dark, with the right lighting, not to mention Mick not wearing that white dress outfit. Somehow, I can't envision 'Midnight Rambler' as carrying the same power and menace that we witnessed at the Garden if Mick had come out in that costume. New Yorkers would not have put up with that at that time. When the Stones left the stage for the last time and the lights came on, all we wanted was more!

I knew I had to have it too, right then and there. I was dazed, as was most of the audience. I was already a concert veteran, having been to hundreds of shows already. I went to the ladies' room and got on that long, ever-present line to get in. But unlike the other women, I didn't leave. I stayed in a stall with my feet up on the seat (which would become a very common thing within a few years; it wasn't back then). I was kicked out of one bathroom, probably two, but after what felt like an eternity, other fans started filtering into the venue. I still had my ticket stub and I waited until the usher was looking the other way to scam my way down to the floor again. When you do this, you have to be prepared to move when anyone shows up for their seat. I had scouted out an empty seat closer to the front and by the end of the second show, I had made it down to about the third or fourth row. Needless to say, it was worth the wait to see this one all over again.

When it was released, my friends and I went to see *Gimme Shelter*. I don't remember which song it was now but at one point, knowing my story, my friend screamed out, 'Dari... that's your hair!' My face never made it on screen, but my huge head of hair had its own zip code back in 1969 and it shows up for a couple of seconds somewhere in that movie. It's the closest I'll ever be to being a rock star.

MIKE JAHN, *THE NEW YORK TIMES*

Sixteen thousand people stood, stomped and danced while the group played faithful versions of their hit songs, like 'Jumpin' Jack Flash' and 'Under My Thumb'. They also did a rousing Chuck Berry rocker, 'Oh Carol', and several acoustic-guitar blues.

The group maintained its long-standing image of being the sexual balladeers of rock music. Many of their songs have an aggressive, masculine theme, and the lead Stone, Mick Jagger, snarls and howls in the finest man-woman blues tradition.

Throughout the songs, Mr Jagger pranced about the stage, flaunting his hips at the audience like a stoned flamenco dancer. Their set was very successful; an enthusiastic reading of some of a fine group's finest material.

The general concert plan worked less well. The audience waited for more than three hours before the Rolling Stones took the stage. There were three other acts, Terry Reid, BB King and the Ike and Tina Turner Revue, and too much time was wasted between acts.

Still Turner brought on the Stones in a magnetic fashion when she closed her set singing and dancing a soul standard, 'Land Of A Thousand Dances', joined by Janis Joplin.

IAN DOVE, *BILLBOARD*

Commercial success for the Rolling Stones Madison Square Garden's circus was assured – a total two-day, three concert gross of $286,000. The main worries were centred on sound and audience. Nobody need have worried, although the November 28 evening concert got off to a bad start. The opening act, Terry Reid, was inaudible, full of static crackle and screech until the whole show stopped for adjustments.

Really, the fact given that they were recording is no excuse for long delays while technicians work. And this after the concert started one hour and 15 minutes late.

The expensive seats ($8) on the floor of the arena had normal vision cut off during the whole concert by the apparent unlimited ability of people from less expensive areas to wander about looking for the mythical vacant seat. Reid, BB King and Ike and Tina Turner were all heard but rarely seen for long intervals.

The Stones appeared aptly at the witching hour, exactly midnight. They have kicked out all the irrelevant excess and emerged ploughing the narrow furrow of straight up rock music. Lyrics keep a firm grasp on reality, over-inflated images have disappeared for the most part. The simplicity was paired right down for a couple of acoustic guitars – vocal numbers – Blind Willie Jagger and Brownie Richards.

Former road manager, Ian Stewart, who used to be called the sixth Stone, came on strongly in several numbers with his bluesy piano... and a white tail suit!

But impressive is the word for the whole fist-clenched audience rising to yell 'Satisfaction'. People are the ultimate spectacle.

29 NOVEMBER 1969

BOSTON GARDEN
BOSTON
MASSACHUSETTS

"'Midnight Rambler' is a song Keith and I really wrote together. We were on a holiday in Italy. In this very beautiful hill town, Positano, for a few nights. Why we should write such a dark song in this beautiful, sunny place, I really don't know. We wrote everything there, the tempo changes, everything... I'm playing the harmonica in these little cafés, and there's Keith with the guitar"

MICK JAGGER

CINDY BABAIAN

I turned 16 just six days before I saw them in '69. I went with a neighbour friend. The show just blew me away. I had never really been to a big concert like that before. I had great seats overhanging the stage and I could not believe what I was seeing.

JEN FORSBERG

I was barely 13 and my brother barely 14 when we saw the Rolling Stones in Worcester, Massachusetts in April 1965. My sister who also attended had just turned 16 and brought her friend, also 16, and her 14-year-old brother. We were dropped off and went up the endless steps into the Auditorium. This was my first concert and all the sounds, sights, emotions and feelings of anticipation left me breathless, anxious and physically excited. After we found our seats, my sister and her friend disappeared. Although I was curious it just seemed like another chaotic thing that can happen at a concert.

The noise was deafening, several thousand kids, mostly girls, all yelling in unison. Then above all that din there was loud screaming and sobbing from a single girl and when I looked down the aisle behind me, I saw my sister and her friend being led back to their seats next to mine by two security guards.

At first, I thought she had been hurt, but she was just hysterical. As it turned out they were two of the four girls that had hid out in the Auditorium garage and jumped the Stones. My sister could barely talk but had scratched Mick's hand and grabbed his shoulder. A girl ran up to my hysterical sister, saying, 'Can I touch you? Can I touch you?'

In 1969 I saw the Stones again at the Boston Garden with my best friend and our boyfriends. Although it was a longer concert and much, much bigger and very exciting, it didn't come close to matching the Worcester concert, which had a more innocent air about it.

LINDA MARKHAM

My boyfriend at the time was an amateur photographer. He took a great photo of Mick in his top hat!

PAM BRALEY

I saw them in Worcester, Massachusetts with Brian. I was 14 years old. I went with five friends from school. We were on the third row, very close to the stage. We could hear the music. I remember Brian was dressed much better than the others, wearing a suit with a white turtle-neck sweater. He played his white Vox guitar and tambourines. Mick didn't move around as much as he does today. The place was not packed; there were a lot of empty seats. I think they were just starting to get some attention in the States. I took pictures, including some good ones of Brian and Mick, but let a friend borrow them and never got them back. I saw them again in Boston in November the same year. That was a bigger concert than the Worcester one.

The last time I saw them was November 29, 1969. There was a lot of open marijuana smoking amongst the crowd, and concerts were changing so much. I never went back to see them again, because I didn't like them without Brian. They never sounded the same without him. He gave the Stones a unique sound with all the instruments he played. I don't think they have really ever given the guy his due credit. I absolutely loved their earlier music.

DIANE STRAUSS

In 1964, the Beatles swept through the United States. Everyone was talking about them. Their music was so fresh, so new, so different. They were also handsome, witty, and charming. America fell in love with the Beatles.

But they were only a small part of what was referred to as the British Invasion. Unbeknownst to me and most of America, during the early 1960s young British musicians were buying up records of American blues artists, studying their style, writing similar blues-based tunes and, in the process, creating an entirely new sound. And these bands were coming to America, playing back to us our very own music. One young band that caught my ear was the Rolling Stones. The Stones were very unlike the Beatles. They were not handsome or charming, but they could crank out blues-based rock and roll like no other band of their time.

My first album was *December's Children*, purchased when I was ten years old. At that young age, I had found the music that spoke to me. They were then, and still remain, my favourite group. I've seen them in concert fourteen times. But of all the tours, the most outstanding was their tour of America in 1969. The Stones packed twenty five shows into one month on the road. Accompanying them were Ike and Tina Turner, BB King, Chuck Berry and Terry Reid. These four powerhouse acts worked perfectly with the music the Stones were playing at the time. On a rotating basis, typically two of the four would open for any one show. They were all big name acts on their own so as a line up, Ike, Tina, BB, Chuck and Terry really gave the tour its punch and sparkle.

I was a month away from my fourteenth birthday at the time and had never been to a live event such as this. What an opportunity to see my favourite band in person. Accompanying me were my two friends from high school, Sheila and Cheryl. Tickets in our hot little hands, we made the hour-long trip to Boston thanks to Cheryl's brother-in-law who kindly gave us a lift. Along with my ticket, I brought the only camera I owned, my father's World War II-era bellows medium format camera, and my Craig 212 portable reel-to-reel tape recorder.

The Rolling Stones played two shows. We had tickets for the (early) 5pm show. Our seats were on the first loge level, on the side, but far from the stage. We wouldn't have a close-up view, but we would be comfortable.

Announcing the acts was road manager Sam Cutler. First on stage was Terry Reid, accompanied by his band. Honestly, he knocked me out. What a phenomenal performance. I wish I had recorded his entire set, but I had only prepared to record the Stones. However, I was so impressed that I turned on the tape recorder and caught the last four minutes of his song 'Superlungs'. I believe he also performed 'I've Got News For You', a nice bluesy number, right up my alley.

BB King had a stellar reputation as a blues musician and I was looking forward to seeing him perform with Lucille, his custom Gibson guitar. But for some reason, he didn't make the show. His backup band came onstage for a quick set, but I was uninterested.

And then, ladies and gentlemen, the greatest rock and roll band in the world. Hysteria swept over us, three girls in our early teens. Screams, giggles, sighs can all be heard on my recording as the Stones took the stage. After a few minutes, we got a hold of ourselves and sat back to watch the show.

Several months earlier, my favourite member, the beautiful Brian Jones had died in a tragic accident in his swimming pool. This was my first look at his replacement, Mick Taylor. The stage was bare, except for the row of Ampeg amps behind the band. Mick, Keith, Mick T, Bill and Charlie, accompanied by Ian Stewart on piano, performed a good mix of old and new tunes. They were so young, just in their early twenties, but they had clearly perfected their style on stage. True professionals, dynamic performers, and in their prime, they needed nothing more than the music to make a big impression on the Boston crowd. Just an hour and fifteen minutes later, Mick threw confetti out of his top hat and the show was over.

My photos and audio recording have survived through the years. Speaking with a friend who collects live concert recordings, I casually mentioned that I had the Stones on tape from 1969. 'What? WHAT!' After composing himself, he filled me in on the historic value of what I possessed. Each recording is unique, like a fingerprint. So although there may be other recordings of this show, there is none the same as mine. He connected me with a company that specialises in analogue to digital transfers, so I sent them my tapes, held my breath, and exhaled several months later when my tapes were returned safely, along with a digital copy.

From there I created a YouTube channel to post this vintage recording, along with several other shows of that era. Although I released the recording for free trade, anonymous bootleggers made short work of it, releasing it for sale on CD. Coincidentally, the back cover of the CD features a photo taken from the rear of the Boston Garden. Captured in the lower right of the photo are myself, Sheila and Cheryl, watching the show and having the time of our lives.

30 NOVEMBER 1969

WEST PALM BEACH MUSIC & ARTS FESTIVAL
PALM BEACH
FLORIDA

"The promoter came up with the idea of having a church service on the Sunday morning that was run by a hippie minister"

KENNETH DAVIDOFF

Headed up by the Stones, the festival line-up also includes Janis Joplin, Sly & The Family Stone, Jefferson Airplane, The Byrds, Steppenwolf, Spirit, Country Joe & The Fish and Johnny Winter.

KENNETH DAVIDOFF

Not too many festival venues had the Rolling Stones; they usually played by themselves or with one other band. But this was a festival show and they were the closing act.

I was the official photographer for the festival. I was real lucky. I grew up in photography. My dad was a professional photographer and in 1955 we moved to Palm Beach and he established himself here. A few years after he started, he photographed Rose Kennedy, the picture went in the newspaper and Rose Kennedy liked the photograph so much that from then on, she always called my father. He became like the Kennedys' family photographer when they lived in Florida.

My dad got me my first camera when I was eight years old. It was a twin lens reflex camera. You're looking down through one lens, but you're taking the picture with the lens below it. When I became a professional photographer, that's what I shot with, a twin lens reflex; my dad was planning for the future. I started working for him when I was 16, in 1966 in Palm Beach.

It was mostly high society, celebrities and very high government officials. I photographed seven presidents, I photographed Charles and Diana, I photographed the launch of Apollo 11, I photographed the 1972 Democratic and Republican conventions. And this is all because I grew up working in my dad's studio. But I was a hippie, I was into rock and roll, and so the first big concert I ever really shot was the Miami Pop Festival in May 1968. It was promoted by Michael Lang (later famous for doing Woodstock) and Rick O'Barry and the headliner was Jimi Hendrix. And I used that leverage when I called to get the Stones gig.

I was with a buddy of mine, and we were listening to the radio and heard that the festival was coming to Palm Beach. I found out who the promoter was and called him and said, 'Look, I'm your guy. I just photographed Jimi Hendrix at a rock festival, I know what I'm doing.' Not that I really did, because I was only 19. But I had progressed a little bit from using a flash, when I photographed Jimi, to being able to shoot with stage lighting, so I got the job as an official photographer for the Palm Beach Pop Festival. And I called the studio and told my dad and my mom; it was all family business.

The festival had a lot of difficulties; the whole town was against it. The religious right thought, 'Oh my God, there's going to be drugs *and* rock' and so the promoter faced quite a few challenges besides the normal ones he'd face putting together a festival. And on a Sunday too. He came up with the idea of having a church service on the Sunday morning that was run by a hippie minister by the name of Reverend Arthur Blessitt.

They set up a Jesus tent and you could go there anytime you wanted to just hang out and talk to people about Christianity. Plus, they had services on the Sunday morning, so the town let the promoter hold the festival because of that. And he hooked up with one other local minister who sort of helped him with the town council and stuff.

The festival was held over three days – Friday, Saturday, Sunday – and we had pretty much every rock band that played at Woodstock except for Jimi Hendrix. Plus we had the Rolling Stones.

But it rained and everything got muddy and bitter cold. We're talking about 40 degrees, which for Florida is cold. And the Stones didn't come on until four in the morning, and it must have been in the mid-30s by then. There were campfires going everywhere so that people could stay warm.

It was all muddy and everything, and my dad was the ultimate Palm Beach photographer. He came out there in his white Gucci loafers. Needless to say, the second time he came out he came out in boots. But he wanted to photograph the Rolling Stones too. We have some really good backstage pictures that my dad took, and I did the performance stuff.

Jefferson Airplane came on right before the Stones and Marty Balin was walking on these wooden planks to keep out of the mud and he was so loaded that he fell right into the mud, and Sam Cutler and the Stones had a big laugh about that.

The Jefferson Airplane finished around one o'clock in the morning and everybody was waiting for the Stones. It was super cold and we were standing around this 80-gallon drum with a fire in it to stay warm.

And there was a lot of controversy about when the Rolling Stones arrived at the festival site; it took them a long time to come on stage. Some people waited for hours. I heard from somebody that it took a long time for them to appear because they wanted to count the money (the cash fee they were receiving) by hand.

Because a lot of people had to go to work the next day, which was Monday. 75 or 80 per cent of the people who went to that festival thinking they were going to see the Rolling Stones went home disappointed, because they had to go to work the next day and they couldn't stay until the end.

I think it took like two or three hours from the time they arrived until the time they actually came on the stage at four in the morning. And by then, so many people had left the festival. There must have been about 50,000 people at the festival to begin with. But by the end, it was only about 5,000 people. So, I think they had heaters on the stage, but it wasn't really enough.

We were in this trailer, like a mobile home kind of a thing, that was, I guess, their green room for the festival, and they sort of camped out there until they were ready to come on stage.

Mick said something stupid like, 'Hello, Miami,' because he didn't know where the hell he was. It was the day after the recording of *Get Your Ya-Ya's Out* at Madison Square Garden. So when they came to Palm Beach they played the full album for us.

I was Googling 'Mick Jagger photos' and came across a site that said '20 most iconic photographs of Mick Jagger'. And a shot I'd taken of Mick was number two on that list. I was very honoured. The Stones had wanted to use it for a tour in Australia on a billboard, but we couldn't come to an agreement.

KATY MCLEOD

And then we went to West Palm Beach Forum for one last show on the tour. It was a festival. Janis Joplin was there. Steppenwolf. The Stones were top of the bill. I met a guy called John Thaines. He was a con man but he told me where they were staying in West Palm Beach and when their plane was going to arrive. He gave me all my intel.

They thought we were with the Rolling Stones because of that button. We got helicopter passes to fly from the airport to the hotel, which was on the beach, on the ocean. And they let us into the Stones' dressing rooms because of that button. It was a silver trailer. But we didn't stay long because we didn't want to get caught. We didn't want Keith to walk in and say, 'Get them out of here.'

2 – 4 DECEMBER 1969

MUSCLE SHOALS STUDIO
3614 NORTH JACKSON HIGHWAY
SHEFFIELD
ALABAMA

"But when the Lord gets ready you got to move"

MICK JAGGER

The Stones record 'Brown Sugar', 'Wild Horses' and 'You Gotta Move', all of which later appear on their 1971 album, *Sticky Fingers*.

KEITH RICHARDS

I thought it was one of the easiest and rocking-est sessions that we'd ever done. I don't think we've been quite so prolific… ever (laughs). I mean we cut three or four tracks in two days, and that for the Stones is going on something! We left on a high with 'Brown Sugar'. We knew we had one of the best things we'd ever done… I always wanted to go back there and cut more, you know? Then shit happened, so we ended up in France in a basement there doing *Exile On Main St.* Otherwise, *Exile* would have probably been cut in Muscle Shoals. But politically it wasn't possible – I wasn't allowed in the country at the time. So, that was that!

EARLY DECEMBER 1969

CALIFORNIA

"The tour has been really good fun – and the travelling has been easy. We've done Baltimore, New York and Philly and we've got used to being on the road again very quickly. It's three years since we did it last, and it's just as exciting and crazy. We've been playing about an hour and quarter shows, and even longer if things go really well. We've been playing well. Mick Taylor is doing fine. We start off with five fast rock and rollers then slow it down for a few acoustic numbers. We've been playing a few tracks off the new album *Let It Bleed* and from *Beggar's Banquet*"

MICK JAGGER

PHILIP ELWOOD, *THE SAN FRANCISCO EXAMINER*

The Rolling Stones are still hoping to perform in a gigantic free show in the San Francisco area on Saturday afternoon. But as of this morning no site had been found for the concert, which certainly would attract 100,000 spectators, and probably more.

Rock Scully, Grateful Dead manager and principal organiser for the homeless Saturday rock extravaganza, commented last night, 'The whole show's production is together. We are a mobile rock festival with no place to go, yet.'

Participants, besides the Stones and Dead, would be the Jefferson Airplane, the Ali Akbar Kahn School, and perhaps Crosby, Stills, and Nash in an acoustic-instrument set. Marin County, as reported here last week, is still the most likely spot for the show.

The five Stones 'may drift into the Bay Area tonight or tomorrow', commented Scully.

They have been recording in Muscle Shoals, Alabama following an appearance in West Palm Beach, Florida, on Sunday night. Sam Cutler, tour manager for the Stones, and Jo Bergman, their personal representative, have both been in San Francisco since yesterday morning.

6 DECEMBER 1969

ALTAMONT SPEEDWAY
ALTAMONT
CALIFORNIA

"Altamont all happened so quickly. It was very surreal, a nightmare, actually. The whole idea of doing a show at Altamont Speedway was an afterthought. We'd finished the tour and were at Muscle Shoals in Alabama, recording 'Wild Horses' and 'Brown Sugar'"

MICK TAYLOR

"I felt great about the '69 tour right from the beginning. The audience were fantastic... We got great reviews. The records were selling really well... We did what? Twenty shows? They were all great up until Altamont"

BILL WYMAN

"It was chaotic beyond belief. The stage was bowed from all the people who were on it. Sixty or seventy people, lots of Hell's Angels, lots of hangers on. All I wanted from the minute I got there was to get out"

ETHAN RUSSELL, PHOTOGRAPHER

"There was no love, no joy at Altamont. It wasn't just the Angels. It was everybody. In 24 hours, we created all the problems of our society in one confined area – congestion, violence, dehumanisation"

UNKNOWN

THE BERKELEY BARB

As if it were an ancient pilgrimage to Jerusalem, they relentlessly pressed on in the cold grey morning to Altamont Speedway. The sheer numbers were staggering – an unbroken line, ten abreast for miles, and as you looked ahead and behind amidst that mass of bodies there seemed to be no end and no beginning.

Many who were unfamiliar with Livermore (which must have been 99 per cent) had parked their cars miles away from the concert, not realizing that ten or twelve miles stood between them and Altamont. Freeways were turned into gigantic parking lots as drivers tired of waiting for traffic to move. Hitchhikers stumbled by roadsides, some having come from hundreds of miles away.

And when the rendezvous was finally reached and you stepped into the arena to be counted among those who were part of the Last Great Psychedelic Electrical Orgasm of 1969, all you could say was 'Holy Shit.' Between 150,000 and 300,000 encircled the makeshift stage, swelling out, up and over the barren hills…

BUCK LACEY

Altamont was a travesty. It was something that just shouldn't have happened at all. It was Sam Cutler's mistake. The Hell's Angels in the UK were kind of a motorcycle club but the Hell's Angels in Livermore, California were a gang and drug dealers. It was a big mistake for Cutler and Melvin Belli, who was the lawyer on the scene, to get those guys in there.

At the beginning of the documentary about Altamont, there's a black guy that comes up to the stage and he lays it right out. They were setting up and he said, 'Hey, you guys, you don't know what's going on here. This is going to be terrible. You got all these people and you have the Hell's Angels.' And that guy was a really good friend of mine. His name was Sam Steverson and he was a teacher. I look at the sixties as very dysfunctional for everybody, but also very enlightening.

JOE PRUSS

Brian Jones had died on 3 July 1969 and the Rolling Stones did a free concert in Hyde Park, London as a memorial. Aware of the cultural success of Woodstock, there were rumours the Rolling Stones would do a free concert in America when they toured in the fall of 1969.

In the San Francisco Bay Area, underground radio was where my crowd would listen to long format music. It started with long-time AM pop music Bay Area DJ 'Big Daddy' Tom Donahue on radio station KMPX but moved to KSAN by 1969. KSAN was literally the only station we listened to for the newest music, often enjoying late night listening parties when they played, without interruption, new records before their official release.

On Wednesday, December 3, 1969, KSAN announced a Rolling Stones free concert at Sears Point Raceway, on December 6, 1969, in Sonoma, California, north of San Francisco. Cheryl heard this announcement and we started to make plans for the two-hour drive from where we lived in Livermore to Sears Point. Due to permit and contractual difficulties, and the day before it was scheduled to take place, the free concert was moved on December 5, 1969 to Altamont Raceway in Livermore, California, literally 20 minutes from our home on Almond Avenue.

I was working at Rod's Hickory Pit as a dishwasher. Rod, a conservative, was not a fan of the Rolling Stones. When I asked to get off early on the Friday night to go early and camp outside the gate for the show on Saturday, Rod said 'no!' I quit on the spot. Cheryl picked me up early to meet up with our friend Richard, who knew a backroad shortcut to the entrance of Altamont Speedway.

It was around 10pm when we arrived and parked maybe a quarter mile from the entrance. There were already California Highway Patrol announcements about the backup on Interstate Highway 5 and illegal parking on the highway. Richard's backroad route had avoided the backups and we were greeted by many campfires and young people offering drugs, particularly LSD. I don't remember sleeping that night. (Oh, to be 18 years old again and be able to stay awake all night and still party the next day!)

Around 7am on December 6, 1969, the day of the show, the Altamont Speedway fence came down and those of us already congregating at the entrance rushed in and ran to where the stage was, at the bottom of a large bowl. Cheryl and I, now separated from our friends, positioned ourselves on a large blanket, staking out our space, maybe 30 feet from the stage, right behind the roped off front.

Around this time, we took our first hit of LSD. It was everywhere! I remember going to the porta-potties behind the stage where every other interaction was an offer of free LSD. There was so much of it going around that the public address system was making announcements from the San Francisco Haight Ashbury Medical Clinic as to which LSD to not take and avoid a bad trip. I remember announcements to not take the brown LSD!

Our position so close to the front started out great but later became problematic due to the last-minute venue change, the Hell's Angel security, the stage being built only three feet off the ground, the lack of organisation and the LSD.

The concert began with Santana at 2pm. They were local to San Francisco and played almost every festival in the Bay Area and we had seen them several times before. They had a lot of energy and started before the concert bowl was packed, so we were still able to protect our space.

Around 3pm I made another trip to the porta-potties behind the stage and walked by a small trailer with Keith Richards on the step speaking to a reporter.

Wikipedia and others say that the Jefferson Airplane were up next but Cheryl and I remember it as the Flying Burrito Brothers. I'm guessing it was around 3pm. We were really looking forward to them as Cheryl had introduced me to their debut *Gilded Palace Of* Sin record a few months earlier. We remember hundreds of frisbees being tossed above the crowd during their set, and the Flying Burritos given a more light-hearted hippy reception from the audience after Santana's high-octane set. The sound wasn't the best during their set and we had difficulty hearing Gram Parson's voice.

Things were already getting weird for us and the crowd. Our protected blanket space was getting smaller and smaller as the crowd grew and pushed forward to the stage. The rope in front of us went down around the time the Burritos came on. There was a giant Great Dane sitting behind us that had a drooling problem, drooling on both of us. And there was a big commotion coming towards us from behind. When we got up, we saw it was Mick Jagger with bodyguards making his way through the crowd when someone swung a punch and hit him in the mouth! There was an obese naked man standing and dancing close by.

The Hell's Angels were getting drunk and crazy, riding their Harley Davidson motorcycles through the middle of the crowd and getting upset if anyone touched their bikes. They were clearing the way by beating the crowd with shortened pool cues. They beat the naked obese man until he was laying on the ground. (This memory could also be from the LSD that we were pretty much peaking on at 4pm!)

Next up were the Jefferson Airplane, who had recently released their *Volunteers* record. We were fans and had every record from them. Early in their set, Grace Slick and Marty Balin tried to talk the Hell's Angels into not hitting the crowd by stopping in the middle of their set and Grace Slick saying into the sound system 'easy' and, 'Keep your bodies off each other unless you intend love.'

Being drunk, the Hell's Angels were not interested and seemed to be enjoying beating the hippies. Marty Balin tried to intervene and a Hell's Angel hit him and knocked him out. I remember Paul Kantner screaming into the microphone to the Hell's Angels, 'Thank you, you just knocked out my lead singer!'

About this time, 4.30pm, we were getting crushed by the crowd and were starting to get paranoid from the violence and overall weirdness. We decided we needed to escape this madness and relocate to the back of the concert bowl and watch the show from there.

Sam Cutler, the Rolling Stones road manager, was now doing the announcing and telling fans to get off the scaffolding and stage lights and to stop hitting each other. We pretty much missed Crosby, Stills, Nash and Young, around 4.45pm, even though we had loved their album. We were fighting our way through to the back of the crowd throughout their set.

Once we found a place to sit, close to the helicopter pad, we waited and watched artists leave by helicopter, including the Grateful Dead (who never played) and the Jefferson Airplane.

Things were getting worse with the Hell's Angels and the crowd and the bad acid and there were lots of announcements to get help at the Haight Asbury Free Clinic tent, with more warnings about bad acid and pleas for the Hell's Angels to stop beating hippies with pool cues.

We were glad that we had escaped the craziness and were now on the hill, waiting for the Stones. It was maybe 5.30pm but seemed to take forever for the Rolling Stones to come on with Sam Cutler announcing the familiar, 'Ladies and gentlemen, the Rolling Stones.'

We were now above the fray and did not see the stabbing of Meredith Hunter but from the Altamont movie (*Gimme Shelter*) it appears we would have been next to it had we stayed where we had originally been seated in the crowd. The Stones stopped and restarted several times and Mick was continually shouting 'cool out, people' into the microphone. We stayed on the hill for most of their set but listened to their last few songs, 'Honky Tonk Women' and 'Street Fighting Man' as we exited.

We made it to Richard's car and waited maybe 15 minutes for Richard to show up. We managed to beat the traffic via the backroad shortcut and we were home before 9pm.

Over the next few days, there was a lot of news coverage about the concert. There were radio and TV interviews, with Mick blaming the Hell's Angels for what happened and Sonny Barger of the Hell's Angels blaming the Rolling Stones. The local *Livermore Independent* printed a photo of the crowd on its front page, in which Cheryl and I were clearly recognisable in the middle, at the front of the stage. My mother, who was quite the socialite in 1969, was too embarrassed to let it be known that her son and future daughter-in-law were on the front page of the local newspaper on December 7, 1969 (my 19th birthday) and kept the cutting in her safe!

1969 was a turbulent year in America and Cheryl and I coming of age at that time played a significant role in our future development. 56 years later, in 2025, we look back on so many changes in our world. We started our work careers early and didn't finish college, yet we were able to retire at age 49, enjoying the past 26 years travelling and enjoying so many adventures, including every Rolling Stones North American tour since Altamont and multiple concerts on the last several tours, making new friends in Europe and across America.

We're going through a crazy time right now in America. Someone wrote, 'A Rolling Stones concert is two hours of escape from the craziness of the day.' It's ironic that at Altamont in 1969, we had to escape the craziness before the Stones came on!

ALEX EITELBACH

I'm pretty sure I was married at that time – it was one of those shotgun weddings, but we don't have to get into that right now! So myself, my wife (or girlfriend), Ruth, another good friend, Jimmy McQuiston, and another girl who was an arts theatre major, Chris Hayes, were all living in Laguna Beach. Laguna Beach in the sixties was probably the dope-dealing capital of the United States by leaps and bounds. It was definitely the LSD capital, besides San Francisco. We were all students, going to University of California at Irvine, which had only opened up in 1965. Irvine is about eight or ten miles from Laguna, so we were living the beach lifestyle down at the beach but going to school full-time.

I've been a Stones fan since I first heard them. I distinctly remember in high school, the first record I bought was Bob Dylan, the second was a Rolling Stones record, I think *12 x 5* or whatever their early album was, and then the next was Jimi Hendrix. I was also part of a group that put together the Hendrix Hawaii concert, but that's another story. So anyway, we were big Stones fans.

I knew Chet Helms, who ran Winterland, fairly well. And I knew Bill Graham, who ran the Fillmore. He and I knew each other, but we butted heads more than a few times.

All of us would travel back and forth. We went to San Francisco fairly regularly. There was a time when I was flying up to San Francisco every couple of weeks. Basically, we were students that were involved in the hip lifestyle. I don't want to say 'hippie' because to me, hippies were people that spent most of their time doing nothing. I don't like to say hippies because I've always had money. I liked money. I was successful even when I was a kid. I drove a Mercedes in college. It wasn't like I had megabucks, but I always had money. So the four of us decided to drive up to see the Stones play this outdoor show at Altamont with all these San Francisco bands.

At the time I had a classic VW van. I had tricked out the interior, taken out the seats and made it so like you could sleep in it. It was pretty cool. We decided to go up and I was also going to write an article for the school newspaper. We just took my van, sleeping bags and the kind of food you ate when you were young: bologna, cheese, bread and whatever we drank. I didn't drink alcohol and I didn't smoke, and none of the others did, but we took a lot of drugs. We smoked pot.

No one knew where Altamont was. Everyone's familiar with the city and Berkeley, but these outlying areas were primarily under undeveloped. We just assumed it was like some kind of big valley park-like setting.

Laguna to San Francisco in a VW was about a seven or eight-hour drive. We had a vague idea where it was, but obviously there were no cell phones and no Yahoo Maps. But, somehow, we found it.

I remember the weather was shitty. It was cold and overcast. It wasn't like what we were used to at the beach, where they had concerts at school and these big wooded meadows that were part of the campus. We were used to the Orange County hip lifestyle, which was kind of an elite part of being young and hip.

Laguna was a premier place to grow up and live, right on the beach. One of us was a pretty good surfer. I was a body surfer, you know, that kind of crap. So, I'm just like a kid that grew up at the beach and liked the lifestyle and went to a top school.

So we drove up there and I distinctly remember it because we were so amped; it's like *the Rolling Stones* and it was an open concert. It wasn't like at the Forum or something, where you had to buy expensive seats.

And when we got there, it was either raining or overcast. It was chilly, like in the 50s. I just remember it being kind of crappy and being out in the middle of fucking nowhere. There was no town. It was just this big field. It wasn't even cool like Woodstock; it wasn't like this nice, big, flat glade. I remember there was like a kind of a slight downgrade, slightly angled. And it was open.

There were no obvious bleachers. The stage was set up towards the back. I don't know how many people actually attended, but I just remember it was thousands. It could have been more than 10,000.

You had to find a place to actually park because we weren't going to drive back and stay in hotels. We were young, with a sleeping bag type of deal or whatever, because we were going to be there for two or three days.

Everyone was excited. We're 20 or 21, the hip people from Laguna Beach with all these other hip people from California. We thought everyone was going to be like our type of Laguna Beach thing, where everyone was about peace and love, with all kinds of hot girls and all kinds of cool guys, and everyone liked each other and got along, that kind of thing.

Well, that crowd in Northern California was not a beach crowd. It was composed of all kinds of people, and a lot of lower-class or lower middle-class people that were not part of our normal scene. I'm kind of an elitist, and it probably sounds shitty, but it wasn't our crowd. We were kind of scoping that out.

The thing is, we wanted to see when they were going to start the music and this and that. And then, having found a place to park, we went out and we needed to find a place to actually sit and watch this.

It was pretty packed but I remember we found a place, maybe 50 yards from the stage. It wasn't a big stage like they have today, but it was a raised stage. They had the amps. I don't think there was any light show like those things they used to do in that area, like moving bowls of oil around to produce that kind of spacey stuff you got in those early kinds of light shows.

There were no towers or anything like that, but the stage was fairly large. And, you know, this was like a lot of the big bands that were coming there. But obviously it was the Rolling Stones.

So we found a place to sit and there were all these people, everyone was amped up for the music. And, of course, people were getting high. I'm sure we were smoking joints, but I didn't drop acid. I typically would drop acid when I was in my environment, like at the beach. I've done nutty stuff like driving LSD. I was the guy that always drove to LA. I could drive on acid. No one else could.

I don't remember dropping acid, at least not the first day. We wanted to check it out, not be completely out of it. We were sitting in this area of maybe a couple of hundred or three or four hundred yards on a slight decline. And then it raised up toward the road and there was maybe a hillock or something. It wasn't like a bowl. It was just kind of like a downgrade of this empty shit. You know, the whole thing was weird.

It wasn't our type of deal. We sat down and we were all talking and chatting, and I remember turning my head and there was this big fucking fat guy who was completely naked. He must have weighed two hundred and fifty to two hundred and eighty pounds and he was walking over everyone. It wasn't like, 'Oh, pardon me.' He was obviously out of it. This big hairy fucker walking down toward the stage like that is one thing that has stuck in my mind distinctly.

The other thing was that we pretty soon found out that the security was the Hell's

Angels. I've never been involved with bikers, even though I was a motorcycle rider for a long, long time and had a lot of bikes. The Angels had a shitty reputation. They weren't friendly. They were just this bunch of bad ass bikers who drank, took drugs and beat people up. That was their MO, that and doing crime. It wasn't disturbing at first but it was like 'who the fuck would do that?' You know, have the Hells Angels there? What kind of security could they provide?

And then, later on, everyone who was within a certain distance of the stage saw the altercation, when one guy stabbed that black kid after he pulled a gun (which was idiotic). Before that happened, the Angels were walking around basically shoving people away from the stage, men or women, hitting them. Some of them had like Billy Club-type things. I didn't see any guns, but there were no cops, no highway patrol or any of that stuff.

I can't remember which band started out but the weather got crappier. And I think the Airplane were on stage and one of the Airplane (Marty Balin) got punched by a Hell's Angels. I remember seeing the Angels pushing and acting like thugs, which was exactly what they were. They were fucking thugs, period. I guess they still are.

So as the music started, right away the vibe changed. When you go to a concert, you're amped up, you want to rock out, you want to hear a great band, you want to dance, you want to party, you want to feel good. And you don't want to feel, 'Hey, this is not right,' or 'I'm nervous,' or, 'What the hell is going to happen?' But the vibe changed. And the weather was shitty. And we're out in the middle of fucking nowhere.

The vibe changed with these Angels behaving like that and then band members getting hit. You know, you might see a person get on the stage who was excited. But you don't see people being clubbed down, and these people, these bikers, were violent. You know, that's their MO. They're not like police. They just would hit people. 'Push him, hit him.' And then when I saw that with the guy from the Airplane, I'm thinking, 'Oh, this is out of control.' And I think Bill Graham or someone like that had come out and they were trying to start the music. But it deteriorated from there.

And then, when the Stones finally got in there, they were way off. The sound system was terrible. It wasn't like stacks of Marshalls. Jagger was obviously going 'let's beat it' kind of stuff. I just remember that when the Stones played, the whole thing got more raucous, but in a bad way. I don't remember exactly when we decided that maybe this was enough. And, you know, the next day when we left, I don't remember all that.

You're excited, you're young, you're hip, you've got drugs, you're healthy, you have no cares in the world. And you go up there to party and it turns into this violent fiasco. In that era, hardly anyone got in fights. You know, I got in fights in high school. But when I was in Laguna, it was rare that people would hit each other. It was against the hippie ethic, that kind of crap. But it just changed and deteriorated. And on top of that you had the crummy weather. California, when it's grey, is unattractive. And the Bay Area gets a lot of chill from the ocean.

This headliner, they should have had some power there. There was no control. You know what I mean? The Angels were doing whatever they did. And then it just changed, with bands leaving the stage. I don't know if bands continued to play, but it was like the whole thing deteriorated rapidly.

I've been a Stones fan all my life. I regret that Mick Taylor dropped out. He hasn't done shit in 40 years. He's gotten fat. He looks like an idiot.

I've met Richards and Jagger in New York with a friend of mine who did one of their video tours or a couple of them. I didn't hang with him but, you know, Keith was all right. Mick was like, 'I don't give a fuck – fuck you' type of deal.

DAVID NORWOOD

I was really excited to be going to see some of my favourite bands. I was actually going to see Jefferson Airplane, Santana and The Flying Burrito Brothers. I had seen the Rolling Stones on numerous occasions, including on their first US tour. I had seen The Beatles three times, including their last public performance at Candlestick Park in San Francisco.

I was never a Deadhead. I lived in an area where a lot of the members lived. I coached a Little League Baseball team in the small town I lived in. Rubin Garcia and Jerry's brother Charlie were a part of the team. The day of the concert, I had planned on hitchhiking to Altamont with a friend of mine and I got up that Saturday totally excited to be going. The friend I was going with decided it was 'too big a hassle' for him to go and dropped out. But I was determined and went by myself. I hitchhiked there and arrived sometime around noon.

I found the spot I was going to occupy up on a hill overlooking the stage. I wasn't there 30 minutes when the Hell's Angels started their usual display of bullying and intimidation that is their calling card. I use to run 'errands' for the secretary of the Angels (he also ran a prostitution ring out of his cab) in SF as a teen, which consisted of carrying money and drugs where I was instructed to.

'Bath Tub Beans' was a huge money maker for them. These were counterfeit 'cross tops' (speed, beanies, Black Beauties, etc) that were a form of amphetamine. The bikers would purchase blank tablets, mix chemicals in a bath tub and use a tablet press or stamp to put the cross on the top of the counterfeit pills. You had to take a huge amount of them to get the buzz. This is part of what was bankrolling the Angels. I was given a card with a phone number on it if I ever needed help. All I needed was to give them a call and problem solved.

As I got settled into the spot, the crowd started filling in until the space I had chosen was no longer just a spot but part of a sea of people. My immediate neighbours were two friendly gay guys. We started to share food, alcohol and pot. I asked them to *not* include me in any substance like LSD that we were sharing. They replied, 'Hey man, we wouldn't do that you!' That was cool and I relaxed. We shared stuff all day.

The music got underway and the Jefferson Airplane starting playing but not long into the set, they stopped! They were yelling at the Angels in front of the stage to stop the violence in front of the stage. Next thing I knew they were picking Marty Balin, the Airplane's lead singer, up and putting him on the stage. (I worked with Marty years later and he said he 'remembered' very little of that day.)

A long delay took place while they tried to get things back to normal but the fuse had been lit. The rest of the day was marked by the music starting and stopping due to the violence the Angels were engaged in. I wanted to leave but my spot was so entrenched and surrounded that it would have taken a massive undertaking to get anywhere. The sun beat down on the crowd and the tension was rising.

They kept saying over the sound system that the Rolling Stones were on their way. They finally arrived and the anticipation went up in the crowd.

The sun was going down and I figured the Stones were waiting for nightfall. It was fairly hot that day for Northern California and I felt very dehydrated, so my neighbours gave me some water and wine they had brought with them. I should have known, because the wine was in a jug. As nightfall came about, the Rolling Stones came on and sooo did I! I was pissed. I have taken LSD quite a bit and knew the signs as well as the effects. I was yelling at my neighbours but they thought it was funny. I did not.

The Stones start playing and I could see the area in front of the stage in constant upheaval. Mick had to stop numerous times and ask that the violence stop. They got to 'Under My Thumb' and things went off the rails. The bikers were going crazy beating people up close to the front of the stage. It looked like a mosh pit but you could see the bikers wailing away on people.

The Angels loved shortened pool sticks as weapons. Things came to a halt and there was a long delay while they got the stabbing victim out of the crowded area. That was it for me! I was getting out of there no matter what.

I thanked my neighbours for dosing me and told them that there was a special place in hell for the likes of them. I was stoned out of my mind, stumbling through a tightly packed sea of people in the dark. I had a sense of where I had come from the freeway and headed in that direction. There were barb wired fences, cattle roaming, and Hells Angels riding their bikes across the surrounding fields. All you could see was their headlights flashing all over the place. They were trying to run people down as well. It was like escaping from 'a prisoner of war camp' in World War II. I fought my way to the freeway thinking I was safe and all was good.

I got to the freeway along with thousands of people who were fleeing in cars, trucks, motorcycles and on foot. I was hitchhiking! As far as I could see, so were thousands of other people, all lined in both directions.

I decided that I would not be getting out of there for hours and hours. I was totally desperate and high as hell. I walked along with the complete chaos of a mass retreat of fleeing people! I walk stunned at what the situation was. I would never be able to get a ride with that many people hitchhiking. I walked past a guy getting into a panel van with a couple of people. I went up to him and explained that I had been dosed and needed his help. I said I would quietly sit in the back of his van and be no trouble, 'Nope I am not taking you.' Second request: 'I really need your help.' 'Nope I am not taking you and quit asking me.' Third request. ' I am in really bad shape and need the kindness of another human being to help me! Please I am begging you!' He finally relented and let me get in! He said he didn't want to hear from me on the way back to SF which was 50 miles. I quietly sat in the back in the dark just thanking the universe for allowing me to escape a very dangerous situation.

We drove back in silence as they were as stunned as I was by everything that had happened. They took me to San Francisco and dropped me off close to friends.

It took me days to recover mentally, emotionally and spiritually. I stopped listening to the Rolling Stones and always blamed them for the goat rope called Altamont. I do understand that many forces were at work that day and the Stones thought they were doing the right thing.

I have had a lot of experiences with the Angels and knew what to expect. They performed as I knew they would.

MARCUS MONTE CHRISTO

I was 13 years old and I hitchhiked there. I remember an immense crowd. Sitting far from the stage the sound was terrible. CSN&Y were okay but I was there for the main event, the Stones, who took the stage well after dark. During the day I took a pill of THC and felt euphoric but I was back down to earth by the time the Stones came on. I could make out Mick dancing in black with a purple cape. The song was 'Midnight Rambler', but Mick kept stopping the number to address the crowd. I had no idea about the violence… Somehow, I made it back home to Marin County.

MIKE WISEMAN

Shortly after the Stones appeared at the Oakland Coliseum Arena, I was riding home across the San Mateo Bridge when I heard The Beatles had broken up. This was right around the end of November in 1969. Shortly after that, I heard that the Rolling Stones were thinking of presenting a free concert in the Bay area. I can't think the two events were unrelated. Here were the Stones, the last group standing from the British Invasion, and it seemed only natural that they would want to celebrate their being the last of the two rock groups who could be considered the best.

At first, the concert was scheduled for Sears Point Raceway, a place up above the Bay Area kind of close to Santa Rosa, but then a few hours later it was said that the planned concert was rejected by the county in that area. I stayed tuned to the radio to listen for updates. Shortly after that, it was rescheduled for the Altamont raceway, which was about 20 miles from the greater Bay area, closer to Tracy, California than the San Francisco and Oakland urban area.

My girlfriend and some of my closest friends attended the Altamont concert with me. We sat back about a hundred yards from the stage and we had no problems. But we could see constant interruptions from the crowd near the stage, which kept on pushing forward. This was not a crowd that was willing to be peaceful and loving and compromise. This was a crowd of people that thought that they were entitled to sit closer to the stage than you, and they were willing to push their way in to do it.

Unfortunately, they also pushed over the Hell's Angels bikes repeatedly and got beat up for doing it. By the end of the day, the Hell's Angels were clearly pissed off at the crowd and they were unable to keep the crowd under control while the performers were on stage.

When the Stones finally came on, the Hell's Angels were still doing their job. Meredith Hunter pulled a gun and waved it in the direction of the stage. One of the Hell's Angels, Alan Passaro, stabbed him and killed him. I can't believe that Passaro did not save somebody's life by doing that.

We heard all kinds of negative press blaming the Stones and the Hell's Angels, and everybody but those that I thought were responsible, which was the crowd itself. I can't imagine what would have happened if the Hell's Angels hadn't been there. Regular uniformed security guards would have been overrun and the stage would have been torn down. The Hell's Angels actually did a great job of containing that audience.

NEIL BLACKFIELD

Altamont Speedway was a race track in eastern Contra Costa County about 56 miles or so east of San Francisco. The racetrack was not the first or second or third choice for this free concert organised by the San Francisco bands Jefferson Airplane and the Grateful Dead.

Their first choice for this western Woodstock was in Golden Gate Park in San Francisco but the 'powers that be' in SF made it too hard. Finally, the owner of the Altamont Speedway said to use his racetrack after a number of other locations did not work out.

300,000 people showed up. The first mess was that with so many people and cars we had to leave our car on the side of the road and take a long walk from the highway to the racetrack. Now it could have been okay, but for some weird reason the Dead kinda hired the SF chapter of the motorcycle club (read 'gang') the Hell's Angels to provide security around the stage. And that is probably why the concert went downhill pretty fast.

What I remember is that the Hell's Angels started drinking right away and throughout the concert they were on the stage throwing full cans of beer into the crowd and pushing and punching anyone that came too near them on the stage.

I was seating on the grassy hill in the middle of the crowd, about 30 yards from the stage. The Angels just kept drinking and being mean to everyone. They even beat up the Jefferson Airplane's singer Marty Balin when he tried to stop them from beating on a person near the front of the stage. What a mess.

Finally, right after it got dark the Stones came on and their thing. That was nice, but I don't think my friends and I stayed for the whole set as we had a long walk in the dark to find our car and get out of there before the traffic jam was too much.

ROBERT 'BERTO' FERREIRA

In 1969, I was living on Bluebird Canyon Drive in Laguna Beach. In the evenings I was working the light show at a popular rock 'n' roll club called Finnegan's Rainbow in Costa Mesa. Finnegan's was Orange County's main destination for listening and dancing to live psychedelic music. The club had a large wooden dance floor that was usually full of music lovers from the beach communities of Huntington, Newport and Laguna. There were also two pool tables to the side of the dance floor.

Also working at the club was a quite nice cocktail waitress from Huntington Beach whose name was Joy, though her surname escapes me now. I didn't know Joy well because I was usually either upstairs running the light show or out on the dance floor dancing. Joy was a beautiful beach woman, with long natural blonde hair, no or very little makeup, and a smile that would light up the room.

During a band break, Joy and I got to talking about the free concert the Rolling Stones were putting on at a race track in the town of Altamont, east of San Francisco in just a day or two. I'd seen the Stones open this tour in Los Angeles at the Forum and I thoroughly enjoyed their show so I had genuine interest.

Six months earlier I had attended all three days of the Newport Pop Festival in Devonshire Downs and I had an absolute blast, so another large music festival sounded alluring.

Joy and I decided to see if we could make it happen. The next day, I phoned the Orange County Airport and secured a flight for two to San Francisco for the following day, which was the day of the concert. A man named Bobby who often came to the club and played pool approached me and said he was going to give us some cocaine for our trip. I'd never had cocaine as I was solely into pot or psychedelics but I said 'okay'. He told me to drive by his house and he'd leave it in his mailbox, which I did and picked it up for our trip.

The next day, Joy and I headed to the airport in my 1952 MG TD. Upon arrival, we found that our flight had been delayed for about 45 minutes so we decided to go out to my car, drop the glove box door open, roll up a dollar bill and ingest some of our gift. We did a few lines and headed back into the airport. They boarded us on the plane and we both began to feel nauseated. Although we would not discover the true nature of the substance until our return, the 'cocaine' turned out to be pure heroin. Ugh. As our plane took off, we were each holding a barf bag in case we got sick. It was not a pleasant ride but it was only a short flight.

We arrived in San Francisco and it was easy to find a ride to the site with other concert goers. When we arrived at the festival, I'd never seen so many people. It made the Newport Pop Festival look like a garage sale. Each hill, no matter where I gazed, was covered with people. We were still under the effects of the heroin but, thank goodness, it was no longer as strong.

We missed seeing Santana. Jefferson Airplane were finishing up their set as we worked our way toward the stage. We could hear Grace talking about something happening to Marty but we couldn't quite figure out what. The Flying Burrito Brothers had begun their set as we settled into our spot. I'm not sure how we did it but we managed to get fairly close to the right corner of the stage, affording us a reasonably good line of sight to the performers. However, the vibes up front were not good. There was a tension in the air, though that could well have been exacerbated by our coming down from what we had ingested.

Crosby, Stills, Nash & Young were up next, a band that years later would become my favourite band of all time. They were okay but I think most of the performers by now were unsettled due to the Hell's Angels acting as the security and being completely wasted from large amounts of alcohol along with (apparently) LSD.

Then the announcement came introducing the Rolling Stones. This caused the crowd to inch forward and, in so doing, motorcycles that belonged to the Angels began getting knocked over and scuffles began as angry Angels reacted. People that were front and centre were getting pushed forward with little room to move. Though we were close by, we could not tell what was actually happening until Mick stopped singing and began pleading for everyone to calm down and chill out.

Despite the hardships and Mick's pleadings to settle down, the Stones – as always – put on a decent show. When their set ended, we caught a ride back to the airport and headed home. We were exhausted, spent, and landed back in Orange County that same night. Joy stayed with me that night and we slept for a good many hours. We were still kind of spaced out the next few days.

A friend named Sonny came by and tested the substance we ingested. He was the one that determined what it was and said it was the best heroin he'd ever done, at which point I gave him the remainder. Not my cup of tea.

I saw the Stones at State Farm Stadium in Phoenix on their most recent tour. They still have it. They're still the best rock 'n' roll band of my generation.

SARA SPINNER

I went to that show but left before dark so I didn't see the Stones play!

BETH ELLIOTT

My brother and I had it in our heads to ride our bicycles to Sears Point for the free show that got moved to Altamont Speedway. Altamont was too far for us to cycle to. Fate was kind.

BRAD WALKER

I had first seen them on their second US tour, at the LA Sports Arena in December 1965 and I don't remember if they had been to town since. I then saw the Stones in 1969 at the LA Forum, their first paying gig in America for a while. And I saw them close out the decade at the ill-fated Altamont free concert, where one of the Hell's Angels, hired to secure the stage area of the show, would kill a person who waved a starting pistol around, mostly because he was obviously very stoned and the vibe near the front was bad. Despite many interruptions and the very unfortunate death of the audience member, the band showed themselves to be excellent purveyors of their own unique brand of hard rock 'n' roll, much better and tighter than the show I had seen some weeks before in LA.

CHIP MONCK

I first worked with the Stones at Altamont. Jo Bergman, Mick's PA, saw CSNY at the Greek Theatre in Los Angeles, called Mick in Mount Fairy, Australia, where he was filming *Ned Kelly*, and said, 'I found ya your lightman.' I started with them for the 1969 US tour. I was in charge of lighting and production management. Sam Cutler was the tour manager in '69, but I successfully got rid of him after Altamont. Altamont is a story of total failure and everybody thinking about their own little position – Rock Scully, Sam Cutler, Alan Rogan and the Angels. Everybody wanted to get done what they wanted to get done. So there's no facilities, no toilets, no food – and 300,000 people.

7 DECEMBER 1969

ALTAMONT SPEEDWAY
ALTAMONT
CALIFORNIA

"You can put half a million young English people together and they won't start killing each other. That's the difference"

KEITH RICHARDS

"I thought the scene in San Francisco was supposed to be so groovy. I don't know what happened; it was terrible. If Jesus had been there, he would have been crucified"

MICK JAGGER

JEFFERSON MORGAN, *THE GUARDIAN*

Thousands of shivering people awoke this morning in the chilly fog draped around these arid hills, 40 miles south of San Francisco, and continued picking up the pieces in the wake of the largest free rock concert in the history of the western United States. The stragglers had been trapped by the massive three-day traffic jam that resulted when more than 300,000 people went to the Altamont motor racing track for the great alfresco happening yesterday by an appearance of the Rolling Stones.

Four young men had died violently by the time the concert ended last night. The Red Cross, however, reported four births at the raceway. Dozens of people were treated at emergency medical centres for everything from bad drug 'trips' to blisters. By early yesterday afternoon, doctors were forced to send out an emergency call for thorizene, a sedative that mitigates the bad effects of hallucinogenic drugs. Supplies were flown to the site by helicopter from a nearby hospital.

Although the air was filled with the acrid sweet smell of marijuana, the majority of those at the massive encampment comforted themselves with beer and cheap wine. The atmosphere was generally friendly and free-wheeling with people sharing the food and drink they had brought with them. One death was attributed to a knife attack on an unidentified young man by a group of 'Hell's Angels' motor-cyclists. Another youth drowned when he fell into a swiftly moving irrigation canal and two more young men were killed as a car ran over them in their sleeping bags last night.

The concert billed as 'Woodstock West' was originally to be held at Golden Gate Park in San Francisco, the scene of last month's moratorium day peace rally. During swift negotiations after city officials decided they could not handle the expected crowds, the site was shifted first to the Sonoma County wine-growing district north of the city, and finally to this uninhabited moor overlooking the Livermore Valley, where the free use of the automobile track was offered by the owners.

The Rolling Stones were the chief attraction, although the programme included 20 other groups including the Jefferson Airplane and the Grateful Dead. It was the climax of the first American tour for the Stones in three years. Mick Jagger, the lead singer, seemed nervous at first about the size of the audience, but the response soon changed all that. When a young girl broke on to the stage nude during the performance of 'Satisfaction', Jagger stayed well across the makeshift stage until she was hustled away.

KEITH RICHARDS

I thought the show would have been stopped, but hardly anybody seemed to want to take any notice. Oh yes, there were people selling acid. That's the way it is at those free concerts. There are so many people there that the police just stay away – you know, they just try to keep the traffic moving ten miles away. In a way those concerts are a complete experiment in social order. Everybody has to work out a completely new plan of how to get along.

The violence just in front of the stage was incredible. Looking back, I don't think it was a good idea to have Hell's Angels there. But we had them at the suggestion of the Grateful Dead, who've organised these shows before, and they thought they were the best people to organise the concert.

The trouble is it's a problem for us either way. If you don't have them to work for you as stewards, they come anyway and cause trouble. Last week was my first experience of American Hell's Angels. I believe the alternative would have been the Black Panthers. I wouldn't like to say whether they would have been any more vicious.

But to be fair, out of the whole 300 Angels working as stewards, the vast majority did what they were supposed to do, which was to regulate the crowds as much as possible without causing any trouble. But there were about ten or 20 who were completely out of their minds – trying to drive their motorcycles through the middle of the crowds.

Really the difference between the open air show we held here in Hyde Park and the one there is amazing. I think it illustrates the difference between the two countries. In Hyde Park everybody had a good time, and there was no trouble. You can put half a million young English people together and they won't start killing each other. That's the difference.

MICK JAGGER

Some Hell's Angels came to a bar in New York about three months ago to see me. They bought me a drink and said there never was a contract on me, and they apologised. (talking to *The Face* magazine, 1983)

4 SEPTEMBER 1970

GET YER YA-YA'S OUT RELEASED

"Charlie's good tonight"

MICK JAGGER

A live album capturing the Stones live on their US tour is released, using material from the Baltimore and Madison Square Garden shows and with additional vocals overdubbed in Olympic Studios in London in January and February 1970. It's the first live album to top the UK album charts. (It reaches number 6 on the *Billboard* 200.)

The Stones' original concept was for a double album that would also feature selected performances from the various support acts on the tour. Decca nix that idea.

Ya-Ya's is also released in response to what are later estimated to be the sale of 250,000 copies of *Liver Than You'll Ever Be*, a bootleg of the Oakland show from earlier in the tour.

ANTHONY MORGAN

I remember *Ya-Ya's* being released and seeing a couple of songs on TV shortly afterward. I finally bought it and it became a favourite for life. I read about how Decca refused to offer up the planned double album, and thought 'what a shame', until in 2009 and in an admittedly cynical money spinner for whatever actually remains of Decca and ABKCO, it was released with the support acts disc, a pretty pointless video disc, a book and – best of all – a four-track disc that included 'Satisfaction', 'Under My Thumb', 'Prodigal Son' and 'You Gotta Move', which were criminally omitted in 1970. Quite why those four songs couldn't be compressed into the original disc is something that still annoys me.

DAVID MARX

Sarf London, Solipsistic Suave

Ah think I've busted a button on my trousers
I hope they don't fall down
You don't want my trousers to fall down, now do ya?

'Financially dissatisfied, sexually satisfied, philosophically trying,' was Mick Jagger's infamous response to a press conference question as to whether he was 'any more satisfied now' during the Rolling Stones now legendary North American tour of 1969. A cavalcade of shows that had been both promoted and pioneered by sole producer and financial manager, Ronnie Schneider – nephew of Allen Klein. He, who had not only dabbled in The Beatles managerial affairs but had also recently been fired by none of other Keith Richards.

The tour grossed over one million dollars in ticket sales alone which, ranging between three and eight dollars, was at the time, rather unprecedented. There again, the band had on said occasion relocated from playing small/medium-sized theatres into sold-out arenas. This was not only partly due to not having toured North America since July 1966, but a menagerie of subsequent complications such as a repetition of well publicised drug charges. Not to mention the fact that Ike and Tina Turner – who were fan favourites and had reportedly upstaged the Rolling Stones on several dates – Terry Reid and BB King (subsequently replaced by Chuck Berry on assorted shows) were more than mere 'support' acts.

In his review of the shows on 27 and 28 November at New York City's world renown Madison Square Garden, the *New York Times* correspondent Francis X Clines described the traipse through the States as the 'major rock event of the year'. A tour, which in and of itself, could also be characterised as being at the very vanguard of what touring per se, was to invariably evolve into. That of a money, spinning-top induced, musical and pyrotechnic extravaganza, of whom the rock 'n' roll likes of The Who, Led Zeppelin, Humble Pie and indeed Elton John – along with the Rolling Stones themselves – were to make the most of throughout the early to mid-seventies.

Especially when it came to reaping the many reward(s) of ever burgeoning and varying financial accumulation.

Moreover, with a gargantuan swagger par excellence, 'twas most certainly Keith Richards who came away from the band's US tour of '69 with a new found, brazenly idiosyncratic identity. In other words, a solipsistic suave of his own inadvertent, personal design; the ever so defined design of which has since spawned effortless cool unto the stratosphere.

Indeed, prior to the tour, yer Keith was a sarf London, admittedly very slick 'n' more than capable rhythm guitar player; who just happened to look great and co-write the band's ever-increasing catalogue of intrinsic, bad-boy R&B panache. But somewhere amid the tour, Keith mutated into the Jack Daniels-swigging Keef of interstellar, guitar-slinging folklore.

As if on a one-way ticket to some sort of elongated, superlative magic.

Replete with the coolest hair ever known to mankind. Just ask the late, great, Johnny Thunders. Or The Clash's Mick Jones. Or The Pretenders' Chrissie Hynde.

Furthermore, Keef's guitar-slinging co-conspirator in questionable open-chord crime, was the superlative Mick Taylor – of whom, many still agree, accounted for the Stones' most superlative line-up. Having only joined the Stones that June – replacing Brian Jones – and performed just one gig with the band at the free Hyde Park show in London, many still agree that it was the guitar interplay between Messrs Richards and Taylor which accounted for such songs as 'Love In Vain,' 'Honky Tonk Women' and 'Gimme Shelter'.

Just ask Bruce Springsteen, who to this day, remains a huge fan of the latter: 'It was a very important record.' Just as the Rolling Stones jaunt across North America in 1969 was a very important tour, simply because it altered the rock 'n' roll landscape, especially with regards to touring; as the aforementioned likes of The Who and Led Zeppelin were to soon find out.

Is it any wonder the writer Robert Christgau referred to it as 'history's first mythic rock and roll tour'? As it most certainly and undoubtedly was.

And a whole lot more besides.

AFTERWORD

That the 1969 tour of the United States now forms a significant part of the Rolling Stones' legend is indisputable. Altamont capped off a tumultuous year that included Brian Jones' dismissal, Mick Taylor joining the band, Brian's death, the Hyde Park show and Marianne Faithfull's suicide attempt whilst in Australia with Mick Jagger.

But what was intended as a resurrection of the band as a live act and the opening of a new chapter in the band's history with a new guitarist, which would help showcase the material written by the maturing Jagger-Richards songwriting partnership, was beset with problems before the Stones even set foot on US soil in the fall of 1969.

There was pre-tour flak for the ticket prices being charged in 1969, with Ralph Gleason, writing in the *San Francisco Chronicle*, particularly outraged:

Can the Rolling Stones actually need all that money? If they really dig the black musicians as much as every note they play and every syllable they utter indicates, is it possible to take out a show with, say, Ike and Tina and some of the older men like Howlin' Wolf and let them share in the loot? How much can the Stones take back to Merrie England after taxes, anyway? How much must the British manager and the American manager and the agency rake off the top?

Gleason's fury at the prices being charged may have reflected the spirit of the times and a feeling that the Stones weren't digging the hippie ideal and instead were siding with 'the man' in (apparently) exhibiting such corporate greed, but 56 years later the prices being charged do not seem outrageous compared with those being levied in late 2025 to see, for example, Rush on their forthcoming *Fifty Something* tour.

Gleason wrote:

Paying five, six and seven dollars for a Stones concert at the Oakland Coliseum for, say, an hour of the Stones seen a quarter of a mile away because the artists demand such outrageous fees that they can only be obtained under these circumstances, says a very bad thing to me about the artists' attitude towards the public. It says they despise their own audience.

The ticket prices might have seemed outrageous then, but seven dollars would not pay for an hour's parking in downtown Los Angeles today.

And accusing the Rolling Stones of ticket price inflation is nothing new. In December 1963, there was outrage when the admission price for a show at Winchester Lido was reportedly increased from five shillings (25p) to seven and six (37p).

The tour gross for the 26 shows the Stones played was $1,845,728 (according to touringdata.org) with 336,228 tickets sold. The 1981 North American tour, comprising 50 shows, grossed $33,204,882 with 2,081,336 paying customers. Tour numbers since 1981 dwarf even these numbers.

What the 1969 tour also did was set the template for how rock bands would tour in future. Charlie Watts may have bemoaned 'the Led Zeppelin tour' and the need to play for over an hour (in 2023, Paul McCartney laid a similar accusation at Bruce Springsteen for fans expecting three-hour long shows: 'I've told him so; I said, 'It's your fault'), but the Stones brought lighting, production and thought to the pacing and timing of their set list whilst also making the brave move away from performing many of their 'greatest hits'. '(I Can't Get No) Satisfaction', 'Jumpin' Jack Flash' and 'Honky Tonk Women' may have featured prominently in the set in 1969, with 'I'm Free' occasionally being thrown in for good measure, but there was no room for number one singles 'Get Off Of My Cloud' or 'Ruby Tuesday', or for top ten hits '19th Nervous Breakdown', 'As Tears Go By', 'Time Is On My Side', 'Mother's Little Helper', 'Have You Seen Your Mother, Baby, Standing In The Shadow?' and 'The Last Time'. The core of the set was drawn from *Beggar's Banquet* and the yet to be released *Let It Bleed*. The Stones had never been a hits-oriented live act and they weren't about to start becoming one now.

The Stones not only set new standards for concert production (albeit these now seem quite primitive by today's standard, where even the smallest of venues will have computerised lighting displays synchronised to the music being played) but created genuine dramatic tension both from the energy and spontaneity of their performances but also through the lack of a 'guarantee' of an encore.

Today a concert will start and finish at prearranged times, mostly because the venue will have a curfew in place as part of the conditions of its licence, and the encore (or encores) will have been rehearsed and already included on the setlist. In 1969, the Rolling Stones performed 24 shows on the tour and what number they would finish on varied.

The fallout from Altamont – from the contract allegedly taken out by the Hell's Angels on Mick Jagger for supposedly badmouthing the security set up and the Angels' role in it, through to the suggestion that the Stones were to a man responsible for the death of the hippie ideal – cast a shadow over the Stones' career in the early 1970s. Add in the issues the band were having with the Inland Revenue in the United Kingdom, where the tax bill the band was facing was going to leave them broke, and you can understand why the Stones decamped to France for a life of (relative) anonymity and free from hassle. Not that it's easy to remain anonymous when you're Mick Jagger and courting a party-going woman in the shape of Bianca

Perez-Mora Macias (later Bianca Jagger), or when you're Keith Richards and your home in Villefranche-sur-Mer on the Côte d'Azur in France becomes the location for recording the next Stones album and attracts the inevitable circus that follows in the wake of the court of the kings of rock 'n' roll.

The Rolling Stones were to return to North America and tour again in 1972.

ACKNOWLEDGEMENTS

Richard Houghton would like to thank: Wayne Robins (his first published work, at age 19, was the article reproduced on Pages 66-68); Thom Lukas, for permission to quote from his book *A Walk on the Wild Side: The Adventures of a Sixties Teenage Photographer in NYC* (Schiffer Publishing Ltd, 2025); Paul Wood; Bruce Graham; Kate Sullivan.

The Hyde Park section of this book originally appeared in *The Stones In The Sixties – A People's History* (Spenwood Books, 2022).

THE ROLLING STONES 1969 TOUR

BY THE SAME AUTHOR

The Smiths – The Day I Was There
The Jam – The Day I Was There (with Neil Cossar)
Black Sabbath – The Day I Was There
Rush – The Day I Was There
Orchestral Manoeuvres in the Dark – Pretending To See The Future
Shaun Ryder's Book of Mumbo Jumbo
Jethro Tull – Lend Me Your Ears
Cream – A People's History
Queen – A People's History
Thin Lizzy – A People's History
The Rolling Stones in the Sixties – A People's History
Gonna See All My Friends – A People's History of Fairport Convention
All Down The Line
All The Songs Sound The Same (with David Gedge)
Tell Everyone – A People's History of the Faces
This Guitar Has Seconds To Live – A People's History of The Who
Wish You Were Here – A People's History of Pink Floyd
All Our Loving – A People's History of The Beatles
Cropredy Capers – Another People's History of Fairport Convention
The Stranglers – Live (Excerpts)
Jimi Hendrix – The Day I Was There
Sometimes These Words Just Don't Have To Be Said (with David Gedge)
Simple Minds – Heart of the Crowd
Led Zeppelin – Whole Lotta Love – A People's History
Iain Matthews – A People's History

spenwoodbooks.com